Student Solutions Manual for

Statistical
Methods
for Psychology

Fifth Edition

David C. Howell
University of Vermont

D1607126

DUXBURY
THOMSON LEARNING

Australia · Canada · Mexico · Singapore · Spain · United Kingdom · United States

DUXBURY

THOMSON LEARNING

Assistant Editor: *Ann Day*	Cover Design: *Cheryl Carrington*
Marketing Manager: *Tom Ziolkowski*	Cover Photo: *VCG/FPG*
Production Coordinator: *Dorothy Bell*	Print Buyer: *Micky Lawler*
Editorial Assistant: *Jennifer Jenkins*	Printing and Binding: *Webcom Limited*

COPYRIGHT © 2001 Wadsworth Group. Duxbury is an imprint of the Wadsworth Group, a division of Thomson Learning, Inc. Thomson Learning™ is a trademark used herein under license.

For more information about this or any other Duxbury product, contact:
DUXBURY
511 Forest Lodge Road
Pacific Grove, CA 93950 USA
www.duxbury.com
1-800-423-0563 (Thomson Learning Academic Resource Center)

ALL RIGHTS RESERVED. No part of this work covered by the copyright hereon may be reproduced or used in any form or by any means—graphic, electronic, or mechanical, including photocopying, recording, taping, Web distribution, or information storage and retrieval systems—without the written permission of the publisher.

For permission to use material from this work, contact us by
Web: www.thomsonrights.com
fax: 1-800-730-2215
phone: 1-800-730-2214

Printed in Canada

10 9 8 7 6 5 4 3 2 1

ISBN 0-534-38282-7

Table of Contents

General Notes

These solutions were checked using a variety of calculators and computer software. Answers often differ (sometimes a surprising amount) depending on how many decimal places the calculator or program carries. It is important not to be too concerned about differences, especially ones in the second or third decimal place, which may be attributable to rounding (or the lack thereof) in intermediate steps.

Although I do not provide detailed answers to all discussion questions, for reasons given elsewhere, I have provided pointers for what I am seeking for many (though not all) of them. I hope that these will facilitate using these items as a basis of classroom discussion.

Chapter 1 - Basic Concepts

1.1 The entire student body of your college or university would be considered a population under any circumstances in which you want to generalize *only* to the student body of your college or university and no further.

1.3 The students of your college or university are a nonrandom sample of U.S. students, for example, because all U.S. students do not have an equal chance of being included in the sample.

1.5 Independent variables: (a) First grade students who attended Kindergarten versus those who did not. (b) Seniors, Masters, Submasters, and Juniors as categories of marathon runners. Dependent variables: (a) Social-adjustment scores assigned by first-grade teachers. (b) Time to run 26 miles, 385 yards.

1.7 Continuous variables: (a) Length of gestation. (b) Typing speed in words/minute. (c) Level of serotonin in a particular subcortical nucleus.

1.9 The planners of a marathon race would like to know the average times of Senior, Master, Submaster, and Junior runners so as to facilitate planning for handling the finish line.

1.11 Categorical data: (a) The number of Brown University students in an October, 1984, referendum voting For and the number voting Against the university's stockpiling suicide pills in case of nuclear disaster. (b) The number of students in a small midwestern college who are white, Black, Latino, Asian, Native American, Alaskan Native, or Other. (c) One year after an experimental program to treat alcoholism, the number of participants who are "still on the wagon", "drinking without having sought treatment", or "again under treatment".

1.13 Children's scores in an inner-city elementary school could be reported numerically (a measurement variable), or the children could be categorized as Bluebirds ($X > 90$), Robins ($X = 70–90$), or Cardinals ($X < 70$).

1.15 For adults of a given height and sex, weight is a ratio scale of body weight, but it is *at best* an ordinal scale of physical health.

1.17 Speed is probably a much better index of motivation than of learning.

1.19 (a) The final grade point averages for low-achieving students taking courses that interested them could be compared with the averages of low-achieving students taking courses which don't interest them. (b) The quality of communication could be compared for happily versus unhappily married couples.

Chapter 2 - Describing and Exploring Data

2.1 Children's recall of stories:

a.

Children's "and then...s"	Frequency
10	1
11	1
12	1
15	3
16	4
17	6
18	10
19	7
20	7
21	3
22	2
23	2
24	1
31	1
40	1

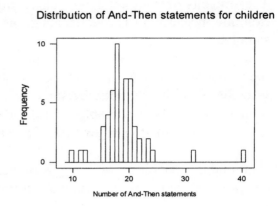

Distribution of And-Then statements for children

b. unimodal and positively skewed

2.3 The problem with making a stem-and-leaf display of the data in Exercise 2.1 is that almost all the values fall on only two leaves if we use the usual 10s' digits for stems.

Stem	Leaf
1	01255566667777778888888889999999
2	000000011122334
3	1
4	0

And things aren't much better even if we double the number of stems.

Stem	Leaf
1*	012
1.	5556666777777888888888889999999
2*	000000011122334
2.	
3*	1
3.	
4*	0

Best might be to use the units digits for stems and add HI and LO for extreme values.

Stem	Leaf
5	555
6	6666
7	7777777
8	8888888888
9	9999999
10	0000000
11	111
12	22
13	33
14	4
HI	31 40

2.5   Stem-and-leaf diagram of the data in Exercises 2.1 and 2.4:

Children		Adults
	0*	1
	0t	34
	0f	55
	0s	7777
	0.	88889999999
10	1*	00000000111111
2	1t	222223
555	1f	4444555
7777776666	1s	667
77777778888888888	1.	
1110000000	2*	
3322	2t	
4	2f	
	2s	
	2.	
40 31	Hi	

2.7 Cumulative frequency distribution for data in Exercise 2-4:

Adult Scores	Frequency	Cumul. Frequency
1	1	1
3	1	2
4	1	3
5	2	5
7	4	9
8	4	13
9	7	20
10	8	28
11	6	34
12	5	39
13	1	40
14	4	44
15	3	47
16	2	49
17	1	50

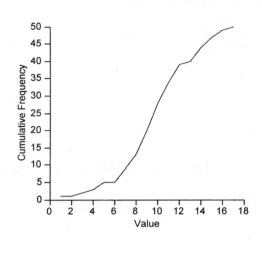

2.9 Invented bimodal data:

Score	Freq
1	2
2	3
3	5
4	10
5	15
6	19
7	16
8	12
9	10
10	15
11	19
12	19
13	16
14	13
15	8
16	4
17	3
18	2
19	1
20	1

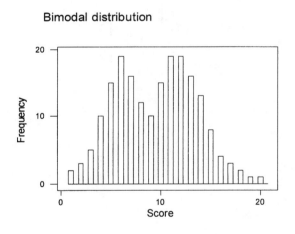

Bimodal distribution

2.11 The first quartile for males is approximately 77, whereas for females it is about 80. The third quartiles are nearly equal for males and females, with a value of 87.

2.13   The shape of the distribution of number of movies attended per month for the next 200 people you met would be positively skewed with a peak at 0 movies per month and a sharp dropoff to essentially the baseline by about 5 movies per month.

2.15   Stem-and-leaf for ADDSC

Stem	Leaf
2.	69
3*	0344
3.	56679
4*	00023344444
4.	5566677888899999
5*	00000000011223334
5.	55677889
6*	00012234
6.	55556899
7*	0024
7.	568
8*	
8.	55

2.17   **a.** $X_3 = 9 \quad X_5 = 10 \quad X_8 = 8$

b. $\Sigma X = 10 + 8 + 9 + \ldots + 7 = 77$

c. $\displaystyle\sum_{i=1}^{10} X_i$

2.19   **a.** $(\Sigma X)^2 = (10 + 8 + \ldots + 7)^2 = (77)^2 = 5929$
$\Sigma X^2 = 10^2 + 8^2 + \ldots + 7^2 = 657$

b. $\dfrac{\Sigma X}{N} = \dfrac{77}{10} = 7.7$

c.   The average, or the mean.

2.21   **a.** $\Sigma XY = (10)(9) + (8)(9) + \ldots + (7)(2) = 460$

b. $\Sigma X \Sigma Y = (77)(57) = 4389$

c. $\dfrac{\Sigma XY - \dfrac{\Sigma X \Sigma Y}{N}}{N-1} = \dfrac{460 - \dfrac{4389}{10}}{9} = 2.344$

2.23 Stem-and-leaf displays:

	1 Stimulus		3 Stimuli		5 Stimuli
3.	678899	3.		3.	9
4*	11122333344444	4*	23	4*	
4.	5555556666667777777889999	4.	666779	4.	6689
5*	111122222333444	5*	00111111122222223333333444	5*	13344
5.	566677778899	5.	55666667888889999999	5.	5555566778888899
6*	1124	6*	00000001111122222223333333444	6*	1111222222333444
6.	6777	6.	5566777799	6.	55555566666777777778899999
7*	112234	7*	22223344	7*	1122444
7.	69	7.	58	7.	566677889
8*		8*	3	8*	11233
8.		8.	6	8.	578
9*	4	9*		9*	4
9.		9.	5	9.	58
10*	44	10*		10*	
10.		10.		10.	
11*		11.		11*	
11.		11*		11.	
12*		12.		12*	
12.		12*		12.	5

As the number of digits in the comparison stimulus increases, the response time increases as well.

2.25 You could compare the reaction times for those cases in which the correct response was "Yes" and those cases in which it was "No." If we process information sequentially, the reaction times, on average, should be longer for the "No" condition than for the "Yes" condition because we would have to make comparisons against all stimuli in the comparison set. In the "Yes" condition we could stop as soon as we found a match.

2.27 For animals raised in a stable environment, there is little or no difference in immunity depending on Affiliation. However, for animals raised in an unstable environment, High Affiliation subjects showed much greater immunity than Low Affiliation subjects. Stability seems to protect against the negative effects of low affiliation.

2.29 There are any number of ways that these data could be plotted. Perhaps the simplest is to look at the change in the *percentages* of each ethnic group's representation from 1982 to 1991.

Change in Ethnic Distribution in U. S. Colleges

1982 to 1991

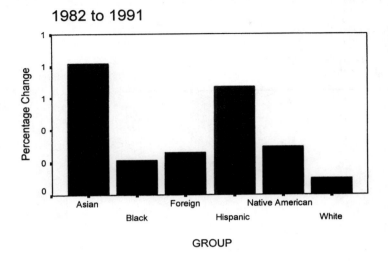

2.31 One way to look at these data is to plot the percentage of households headed by women and the family size separately against years. Notice that there is an uneven sampling of years.

Percent households headed by women

1960 - 1990

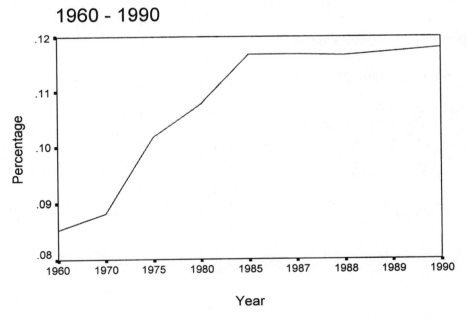

a. There has been a dramatic increase in the percentage of households headed by women over the past 10 years.

b. There has also been a corresponding decrease in family size, part of which is perhaps due to the increase in single-parent families.

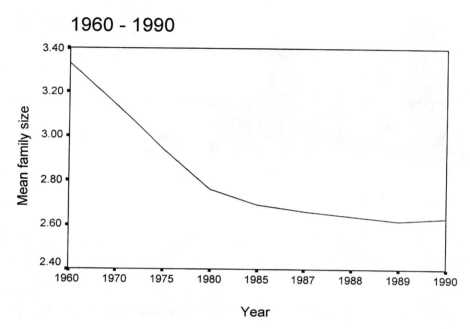

Family size
1960 - 1990

2.33 The mean falls above the median.

2.35 Rats running a straight alley maze:

$$\overline{X} = \frac{\Sigma X}{N} = \frac{320}{15} = 21.33; \text{ Median} = 21$$

2.37 Multiplying by a constant:

Original data (X): 8 3 5 5 6 2 $\overline{Y} = 4.83$
Median = 5
Mode = 5

Transformed data ($Y = 3X$) 24 9 15 15 18 6 $\overline{Y} = 14.5$
Median = 15
Mode = 15

$3\overline{X} = \overline{Y}$ $3(\text{Med}_x) = \text{Med}_y$ $3(\text{Mo}_x) = \text{Mo}_y$
$3(4.83) = 14.5$ $3(5) = 15$ $3(5) = 15$
$14.5 = 14.5$ $15 = 15$ $15 = 15$

8

2.39 Computer printout

2.41 For the data in Exercise 2.1:

$$\text{range} = 40 - 10 = 30$$

$$\text{variance} = s_X^2 = \Sigma\left(X - \bar{X}\right)^2 = (18-18.9)^2 + (15-18.9)^2 + \ldots + (16-18.9)^2$$
$$= 20.214$$

$$\text{standard deviation} = s_X = \sqrt{s_X^2} = \sqrt{20.214} = 4.496$$

2.43 The two standard deviations are roughly the same, although the range for the children is about twice the range for the adults.

2.45 For the data in Exercise 2.4:

The interval:
$$\bar{X} \pm 2s_X = 10.2 \pm 2(3.405) = 10.2 \pm 6.81 = 3.39 \text{ to } 17.01$$

From the frequency distribution in Exercise 2.4 we can see that all but two scores (1 and 3) fall in this interval, therefore $48/50 = 96\%$ of the scores fall in this interval.

2.47 Original data: (reordered)

2	3	4	4	5	5	9	$\bar{X}_1 = 4.57$	$s_1 = 2.23$

$X_2 = 2X_1$:

4	6	8	8	10	10	18	$\bar{X}_2 = 9.14$	$s_2 = 4.45$

$X_3 = X_1/2$:

1	1.5	2	2	2.5	2.5	4.5	$\bar{X}_3 = 2.286$	$s_3 = 1.11$

Multiplying (or dividing) a distribution by a constant multiplies (or divides) the mean of that distribution by that constant. Here we find that the standard deviation of that distribution is multiplied (or divided) by that constant. (The variance is multiplied (or divided) by the square of that constant.)

Adding (or subtracting) a constant to (or from) a distribution adds (or subtracts) that constant from the mean of that distribution. Here we find that the standard deviation of that distribution is unchanged.

2.49 X_2 from Exercise 2.48:   2.381 3.809 1.428 3.809 2.857 4.286 4.286 3.333

If $X_3 = X_2 + c$, then $\bar{X}_3 = \bar{X}_2 + c$, and we want $\bar{X}_3 = 0$

$$\overline{X}_2 = \frac{26.19}{8} = 3.274$$

$$\overline{X}_3 = \overline{X}_2 + C$$

$$0 = 3.274 + C$$

$$-3.274 = C$$

Therefore we want to subtract 3.274 from the X_2 scores:

$X_3 = X_2 - 3.274$: -0.893 0.535 -1.846 0.535 -0.417 1.012 1.012 0.059

$$\overline{X}_3 = 0$$

2.51   Boxplot for data in Exercise 2.4 [Refer to data in Exercise 2.4 and cumulative distribution in Exercise 2.7]

Median location = $(N + 1)/2 = 51/2 = 25.5$
Median = 10
Hinge location = (Median location + 1)/2 = $(25 + 1)/2 = 26/2 = 13$
Hinges = 8 and 12
H-spread = 12 - 8 = 4
Inner fences = Hinges $\pm 1.5\,(\text{H-spread})$

$$= 12 + 1.5(4) = 12 + 6 = 18$$

$$\text{and} = 8 - 1.5(4) = 8 - 6 = 2$$

Adjacent values = 3 and 17

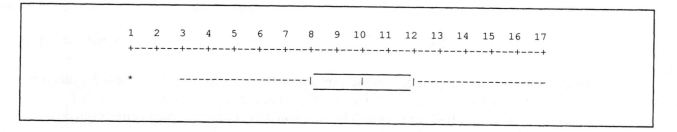

2.53   Coefficient of variation for Exercises 2.1 and 2.4:

For Exercise 2.1 $cv = s / \overline{X} = 4.496 / 18.9 = 0.238$
For Exercise 2.4 $cv = s / \overline{X} = 3.405 / 10.2 = 0.334$

The adult sample shows somewhat greater variability when its smaller mean is taken into account.

2.55   The answers are listed in a file on the disk named BadCancr.err.

Chapter 3 - Normal Distribution

3.1 **a.** Original data:

1   2   2   3   3   3   4   4   4   4   5   5   5   6   6   7

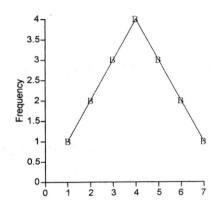

b. To convert the distribution to a distribution of X - μ, subtract μ = 4 from each score:

-3   -2   -2   -1   -1   -1   0   0   0   0   1   1   1   2   2   3

c. To complete the conversion to z, divide each score by σ = 1.63:

-1.84   -1.23   -1.23   -0.61   -0.61   -0.61   0   0   0   0
  0.61   0.61   0.61   1.23   1.23   1.84

3.3 Errors counting shoppers in a major department store:

a.
$$z = \frac{X - \mu}{\sigma}$$

$$= \frac{960 - 975}{15} = -\frac{15}{15} = -1 \quad \text{between -1 and } \mu \text{ lie } \quad .3413$$

$$= \frac{990 - 975}{15} = +\frac{15}{15} = +1 \quad \text{between +1 and } \mu \text{ lie } \quad \underline{.3413}$$
$$.6826$$

Therefore between 960 and 990 are found approximately 68% of the scores.

b. 975 = μ; therefore 50% of the scores lie below 975.

c.   .5000 lie below 975
           <u>.3413</u> lie between 975 and 990
           .8413 (or 84%) lie below 990

3.5 The supervisor's count of shoppers:

$$z = \frac{X - \mu}{\sigma}$$

$$= \frac{950 - 975}{15}$$

$$= -1.67$$

X to $\pm 1.67 = 2(.0475) = .095$; therefore 9.5% of the time scores will be at least this extreme.

3.7 They would be equal when the two distributions have the same standard deviation.

3.9 Next year's salary raises:

a.

$$z = \frac{X - \mu}{\sigma}$$

$$-1.2817 = \frac{X - 2000}{400}$$

$$\$2512.68 = X$$

10% of the faculty will have a raise equal to or greater than $2512.68.

b.

$$z = \frac{X - \mu}{\sigma}$$

$$-1.645 = \frac{X - 2000}{400}$$

$$\$1342 = X$$

The 5% of the faculty who haven't done anything useful in years will receive no more than $1342 each, and probably don't deserve that much.

3.11 Transforming scores on diagnostic test for language problems:

X_1 = original scores	$\mu_1 = 48$	$\sigma_1 = 7$
X_2 = transformed scores	$\mu_2 = 80$	$\sigma_2 = 10$

$$\sigma_2 = \sigma_1 / C$$
$$10 = 7/C$$
$$C = .7$$

Therefore to transform the original standard deviation from 7 to 10, we need to divide the original scores by .7. However dividing the original scores by .7 divides their mean by .7.

$$\overline{X}_2 = \overline{X}_1 / .7 = 48 / .7 = 68.57$$

We want to raise the mean to 80. $80 - 68.57 = 11.43$. Therefore we need to add 11.43 to each score.

$X_2 = X_1/0.7 + 11.43$. [This formula summarizes the whole process.]

3.13 October 1981 GRE, all people taking exam:

$$z = \frac{X - \mu}{\sigma}$$

$$= \frac{600 - 489}{126}$$

$$= .88 \quad p(\text{larger portion}) = .81$$

A GRE score of 600 would correspond to the 81st percentile.

3.15 October 1981 GRE, all seniors and nonenrolled college graduates:

$$z = \frac{X - \mu}{\sigma} \qquad\qquad z = \frac{X - \mu}{\sigma}$$

$$= \frac{600 - 507}{118} \qquad .6745 = \frac{X - 507}{118}$$

$$= .79 \quad p = .785 \qquad 586.591 = X$$

For seniors and nonenrolled college graduates, a GRE score of 600 is at the 79th percentile, and a score of 587 would correspond to the 75th percentile.

3.17 GPA scores:

$$N = 88 \quad \overline{X} = 2.46 \quad s = .86 \qquad \text{[calculated from data set]}$$

$$z = \frac{X - \overline{X}}{s}$$

$$.6745 = \frac{X - 2.46}{.86}$$

$$3.04 = X$$

The 75th percentile for GPA is 3.04.

3.19 There is no meaningful discrimination to be made among those scoring below the mean, and therefore all people who score in that range are given a T score of 50.

Chapter 4 – Sampling Distributions and Hypothesis Testing

4.1   Was last night's game an NHL hockey game?

    a. Null hypothesis: The game was actually an NHL hockey game.

    b. On the basis of that null hypothesis I expected that each team would earn somewhere between 0 and 6 points. I then looked at the actual points and concluded that they were way out of line with what I would expect if this were an NHL hockey game. I therefore rejected the null hypothesis.

4.3   A Type I error would be concluding that I had been shortchanged when in fact I had not.

4.5   The critical value would be that amount of change below which I would decide that I had been shortchanged. The rejection region would be all amounts less than the critical value—i.e., all amounts that would lead to rejection of H_0.

4.7   Was the son of the member of the Board of Trustees fairly admitted to graduate school?

$$z = \frac{X - \mu}{\sigma}$$

$$z = \frac{490 - 650}{50}$$

$$= -3.2$$

z score	p
3.00	0.0013
3.20	0.0007
3.25	0.0006

    The probability that a student drawn at random from those properly admitted would have a GRE score as low as 490 is .0007. I suspect that the fact that his mother was a member of the Board of Trustees played a role in his admission.

4.9   The distribution would drop away smoothly to the right for the same reason that it always does—there are few high-scoring people. It would drop away steeply to the left because fewer of the borderline students would be admitted (no matter how high the borderline is set).

4.11 M is called a test statistic.

4.13   The alternative hypothesis is that this student was sampled from a population of students whose mean is not equal to 650.

4.15   The word "distribution" refers to the set of values obtained for any set of observations. The phrase "sampling distribution" is reserved for the distribution of outcomes (either theoretical or empirical) of a sample statistic.

4.17   **a.** *Research hypothesis*—Children who attend kindergarten adjust to 1st grade faster than those who do not. *Null hypothesis*—1st-grade adjustment rates are equal for children who did and did not attend Kindergarten.

b. *Research hypothesis*—Sex education in junior high school decreases the rate of pregnancies among unmarried mothers in high school. *Null hypothesis*—The rate of pregnancies among unmarried mothers in high school is the same regardless of the presence or absence of sex education in junior high school.

4.19   Finger-tapping cutoff if $\alpha = .01$:

$$z = \frac{X - \mu}{\sigma}$$

$$-2.327 = \frac{X - 100}{20}$$

$$53.46 = X$$

z score	p
2.3200	0.9898
2.3270	0.9900
2.3300	0.9901

For α to equal .01, z must be -2.327. The cutoff score is therefore 53. The corresponding value for z when a cutoff score of 53 is applied to the curve for H_1:

$$z = \frac{X - \mu}{\sigma}$$

$$= \frac{53.46 - 80}{20}$$

$$= -1.33$$

Looking $z = -1.33$ up in Appendix z, we find that .9082 of the scores fall above a score of 53.46. β is therefore 0.908.

4.21   To determine whether there is a true relationship between grades and course evaluations I would find a statistic that reflected the degree of relationship between two variables. (You will see such a statistic (r) in Chapter 9.) I would then calculate the sampling distribution of that statistic in a situation in which there is no relationship between two variables. Finally, I would calculate the statistic for a representative set of students and classes and compare my sample value with the sampling distribution of that statistic.

4.23   **a.** You could draw a large sample of boys and a large sample of girls in the class and calculate the mean allowance for each group. The null hypothesis would be the hypothesis that the mean allowance, in the population, for boys is the same as for girls.

b. I would use a two-tailed test because I want to be able to reject the null hypothesis whether girls receive significantly more or significantly less allowance than boys.

c. I would reject the null hypothesis if the difference between the two sample means were greater than I could expect to find due to chance. Otherwise I would not reject.

d. The most important thing to do would be to have some outside corroboration for the amount of allowance reported by the children.

Chapter 5 - Basic Concepts of Probability

5.1   **a.** Analytic: If two tennis players are exactly equally skillful so that the outcome of their match is random, the probability is .50 that Player A will win the upcoming match.

        b. Relative frequency: If in past matches Player A has beaten Player B on 13 of the 17 occasions on which they played, then Player A has a probability of 13/17 = .76 of winning their upcoming match, all other things held constant.

        c. Subjective: Player A's coach feels that he has a probability of .90 of winning his upcoming match with Player B.

5.3   **a.** *p*(that you will win 2nd prize given that you don't win 1st) = 1/9 = .111

        b. *p*(that he will win 1st and you 2nd) = (2/10)(1/9) = (.20)(.111) = .022

        c. *p*(that you will win 1st and he 2nd) = (1/10)(2/9) = (.10)(.22) = .022

        d. *p*(that you are 1st and he 2nd [= .022]) + *p*(that he is 1st and you 2nd [= .022]) = *p*(that you and he will be 1st and 2nd) = .044

5.5   Conditional probabilities were involved in Exercise 5.3a.

5.7   Conditional probabilities: What is the probability that skiing conditions will be good on Wednesday, *given* that they are good today?

5.9   *p*(that they will look at each other at the same time during waking hours) = *p*(that mother looks at baby during waking hours) * *p*(that baby looks at mother during waking hours) = (2/13)(3/13) = (.154)(.231) = .036

5.11   A continuous distribution for which we care about the probability of an observation's falling within some specified interval is exemplified by the probability that your baby will be born on its due date.

5.13   Two examples of discrete variables: Variety of meat served at dinner tonight; Brand of desktop computer owned.

5.15   **a.** 20%, or 60 applicants, will fall at or above the 80th percentile and 10 of these will be chosen. Therefore *p*(that an applicant with the highest rating will be admitted) = 10/60 = .167.

        b. No one below the 80th percentile will be admitted, therefore *p*(that an applicant with the lowest rating will be admitted) = 0/300 = .00.

5.17   Mean ADDSC score for boys = 54.29, s = 12.90   [Calculated from Data Set]
   a.

$$z = \frac{50 - 54.29}{12.90} = -.33$$

Since a score of 50 is below the mean, and since we are looking for the probability of a score *greater than* 50, we want to look in the tables of the normal distribution in the column labeled "larger portion".

p(larger portion) = .6293

   b.   29/55 = 53% > 50; 32/55 = 58% ≥ 50. (Notice that one percentage refers to the proportion *greater than* 50, while the other refers to the proportion *greater than or equal to* 50.)

5.19   Compare the probability of dropping out of school, ignoring the ADDSC score, with the conditional probability of dropping out given that ADDSC in elementary school exceeded some value (e.g., 66).

5.21   Plot of correct choices on trial 1 of a 5-choice task:

p(0) = .1074	
p(1) = .2684	
p(2) = .3020	
p(3) = .2013	
p(4) = .0881	
p(5) = .0264	
p(6) = .0055	
p(7) = .0008	
p(8) = .0001	
p(9) = .0000	
p(10) = .0000	

5.23 (5 or more correct) = $p(5) + p(6) + p(7) + p(8) + p(9) + p(10)$
                  = .0264 + .0055 + .0008 + .0001 + .0000 + .0000
                  = .028 < .05

5.25   If there is no housing discrimination, then a person's race and whether or not they are offered a particular unit of housing are independent events. We could calculate the probability that a particular unit (or a unit in a particular section of the city) will be offered to anyone in a specific income group. We can also calculate the probability that the customer is a member of an ethnic minority. We can then calculate the probability of that person being shown the unit assuming independence and compare that answer against the actual proportion of times a member of an ethnic minority was offered such a unit.

5.27 Number of subjects needed in Exercise 5.26's verbal learning experiment if each subject can see only two of the four classes of words:

$$P_2^4 = \frac{4!}{(4-2)!} = \frac{4!}{2!} = 12$$

5.29 The total number of ways of making ice cream cones =

$$C_6^6 + C_5^6 + C_4^6 + C_3^6 + C_2^6 + C_1^6 = 1 + 6 + 15 + 20 + 15 + 6 = 63$$

[You can't have an ice cream cone without ice cream; exclude C_0^6].

5.31 Knowledge of current events:

If $p = .50$ of being correct on any one true-false item, and $N = 20$:

$$p(11) = C_{11}^{20} \times 5^{11} \times 5^9$$

$$C_{11}^{20} = \frac{20!}{11!(20-11)!)} = \frac{20!}{11!9!} = 167,960$$

$$p(11) = C_{11}^{20} \times 5^{11} \times 5^9 = 167,960(.00048828)(.00195313) = .16$$

Since the probability of 11 correct by chance is .16, the probability of 11 <u>or more</u> correct must be greater than .16. Therefore we cannot reject the hypothesis that $p = .50$ (student is guessing) at $\alpha = .05$.

5.33 Driving test passed by 22 out of 30 drivers when 60% expected to pass:

$$z = \frac{22 - 30(.60)}{\sqrt{30(.60)(.40)}} = 1.49; \text{ we cannot reject } H_0 \text{ at } \alpha = .05.$$

5.35 Students should come to understand that nature does not have a responsibility to make things come out even in the end, and that it has a terrible memory of what has happened in the past. Any "law of averages" refers to the results of a long term series of events, and it describes what we would expect to see. It does not have any self-correcting mechanism built into it.

Chapter 6 – Categorical Data and Chi-Square

6.1   Popularity of psychology professors:

	Anderson	Klatsky	Kamm	Total
Observed	32	25	10	67
Expected	22.3	22.3	22.3	67

$$\chi^2 = \Sigma \frac{(O-E)^2}{E}$$
$$= \frac{(32-22.3)^2}{22.3} + \frac{(25-22.3)^2}{22.3} + \frac{(10-22.3)^2}{22.3}$$
$$= 11.33^{[1]}$$

Reject H_0 and conclude that students do not enroll at random.

6.3   Sorting one-sentence characteristics into piles:

	1	2	3	4	5	Total
Observed	8	10	20	8	4	50
Expected	5	10	20	10	5	50
Exp. %	10%	20%	40%	20%	10%	100%

$$\chi^2 = \Sigma \frac{(O-E)^2}{E}$$
$$= \frac{(8-5)^2}{5} + \frac{(10-10)^2}{10} + \frac{(20-20)^2}{20} + \frac{(8-10)^2}{10} + \frac{(4-5)^2}{5}$$
$$= 2.4 \quad \left[\chi^2_{.05(4)} = 9.49 \right]$$

Do not reject H_0 that your friend's child's sorting behavior is in line with your theory.

6.5   Racial choice in dolls (Clark & Clark, 1939):

	Black	White	Total
Observed	83	169	252
Expected	126	126	252

---

[1] The answers to these questions may differ substantially, depending on the number of decimal places that are carried for the calculations.

$$\chi^2 = \Sigma \frac{(O-E)^2}{E}$$

$$= \frac{(83-126)^2}{126} + \frac{(169-126)^2}{126}$$

$$= 29.34 \qquad \left[\chi^2_{.05(1)} = 3.84 \right]$$

Reject H_0 and conclude that the children did not chose dolls at random (at least with respect to color). It is interesting to note that this particular study played an important role in Brown v. Board of Education (1954). In that case the U.S. Supreme Court ruled that the principle of "separate but equal", which had been the rule supporting segregation in the public schools, was no longer acceptable. Studies such as those of the Clarks had illustrated the negative effects of segregation on self esteem and other variables.

6.7 Combining the two racial choice experiments:

Study	Black	White	Total
1939	83	169	252
	(106.42)	(145.58)	
1970	61	28	89
	(37.58)	(51.42)	
	144	197	$341 = N$

$$\chi^2 = \Sigma \frac{(O-E)^2}{E}$$

$$= \frac{(83-106.42)^2}{106.42} + \frac{(169-145.58)^2}{145.58} + \frac{(61-37.58)^2}{37.58} + \frac{(28-51.42)^2}{51.42}$$

$$= 5.154 + 3.768 + 14.595 + 10.667$$

$$= 34.184 \qquad \left[\chi^2_{.05(1)} = 3.84 \right]$$

Reject the H_0 and conclude that the distribution of choices between Black and White dolls was different in the two studies. Choice is *not* independent of Study. We are no longer asking whether one color of doll is preferred over the other color, but whether the *pattern* of preference is constant across studies. In analysis of variance terms we are dealing with an interaction.

6.9 **a.** Take a group of subjects at random and sort them by gender and life style (categorized three ways).

b. Deliberately take an equal number of males and females and ask them to specify a preference among 3 types of life style.

c. Deliberately take 10 males and 10 females and have them divide themselves into two teams of 10 players each.

6.11 Doubling the cell sizes:

    a. $\chi^2 = 10.306$

    b. This demonstrates that the obtained value of χ^2 is exactly doubled, while the critical value remains the same. Thus the sample size plays a very important role, with larger samples being more likely to produce significant results—as is also true of other tests.

6.13 Gender and voting behavior

	Vote		
	Yes	**No**	**Total**
Women	35	9	44
	(28.83)	(15.17)	
Men	60	41	101
	(66.17)	(34.83)	
Total	95	50	145

$$\chi^2 = \Sigma \frac{(O-E)^2}{E}$$

$$= \frac{(35-28.83)^2}{28.83} + \frac{(9-15.17)^2}{15.17} + \frac{(60-66.17)^2}{66.17} + \frac{(41-34.83)^2}{34.83}$$

$$= 5.50 \qquad \left[\chi^2_{.05(1)} = 3.84\right]$$

Reject H_0 and conclude that women voted differently from men. Women were much more likely to vote for Civil Unions—the odds ratio is (35/9)/(60/41) = 3.89/1.46 = 2.66, meaning that women were 2.66 times as likely to vote for civil unions than men. That is a substantial difference, and likely reflects fundamental differences in attitude.

6.15 The relationship of assistance-seeking behavior to number of bystanders:

		Sought Assistance		
		Yes	**No**	**Total**
	0	11	2	13
		(7.75)	(5.25)	
Number of Bystanders	1	16	10	26
		(15.5)	(10.5)	
	4	4	9	13
		(7.75)	(5.25)	
		31	21	52 = N

$$\chi^2 = \Sigma \frac{(O-E)^2}{E}$$

$$= \frac{(11-7.75)^2}{7.75} + \frac{(2-5.25)^2}{5.25} + \cdots + \frac{(9-5.25)^2}{5.25}$$

$$= 7.908 \qquad \left[\chi^2_{.05(2)} = 5.99 \right]$$

Reject H_0. The number of bystanders influences whether or not subjects seek help.

6.17 a. Weight preference in adolescent girls:

	Reducers	Maintainers	Gainers	Total
White	352	152	31	535
	(336.7)	(151.9)	(46.4)	
Black	47	28	24	99
	(62.3)	(28.1)	(8.6)	
	399	180	55	634 = N

$$\chi^2 = \Sigma \frac{(O-E)^2}{E}$$

$$= \frac{(352-336.7)^2}{336.7} + \frac{(152-151.9)^2}{151.9} + \cdots + \frac{(24-8.6)^2}{8.6}$$

$$= 37.141 \qquad \left[\chi^2_{.05(2)} = 5.99 \right]$$

Adolescents girls' preferred weight varies with race.

b. The number of girls desiring to lose weight was far in excess of the number of girls who were overweight.

6.19 Analyzing Exercise 6.12 (Regular or Remedial English and frequency of ADD diagnosis) using the likelihood-ratio approach:

	1st	2nd	4th	2 & 4	5th	2 & 5	4 & 5	2,4,&5	Total
Rem.	22	2	1	3	2	4	3	4	41
Reg.	187	17	11	9	16	7	8	6	261
	209	19	12	12	18	11	11	10	302

$$\chi^2 = 2\left(\Sigma O_{ij} \ln\left[\frac{O_{ij}}{E_{ij}}\right]\right)$$

$$= 2 \times [22 \times \ln(22/28.374) + 2 \times \ln(2/2.579) + ... + 6 \times \ln(6/8.642)]$$

$$= 2 \times [22(-.25443) + 2(-0.25444) + ... + 6(-0.36492)]$$

$$= 12.753 \text{ on } 7 \text{ } df$$

Do not reject H_0.

6.21 Monday Night Football opinions, before and after watching:

As the data are originally presented, chi-square would not be appropriate because the observations are not independent. The same subjects contribute twice to the data matrix.

6.23 **b.** Row percents take entries as a percentage of row totals, while column percents take entries as percentage of column totals.

c. These are the probabilities (to 4 decimal places) of a $\chi^2 \geq \chi^2_{obt}$

d. The correlation between the two variables is approximately .25.

6.25 For data in Exercise 6.24a:
a. $\phi_C = \sqrt{26.90/22071} = .0349$

b. Odds Fatal | Placebo = 18/10,845 = .00163.
Odds Fatal | Aspirin = 5/10,933 = .000453.
Odds Ratio = .00163/.000453 = 3.598
You are 3.6 times more likely to die from a myocardial infarction if you do not take aspirin.

6.27 For Table 6.4 the odds ratios for smoking as a function of gender = (150/350)/(100/400) = 1.71. Men are 1.7 times more likely to smoke than women. For Table 6.5 the odds of being the primary shopper as a function of gender = (15/4)/(4/15) = 14.06. Women are 14.06 more likely to be the primary shopper. This gender difference is much more extreme than it was for smoking.

6.29 Dabbs and Morris (1990) study of testosterone.

		Testosterone		
		High	Normal	Total
	No	345	3614	3959
		(395.723)	(3563.277)	
Delinquency	Yes	101	402	503
		(50.277)	(452.723)	
		446	4016	4462 = N

$$\chi^2 = \Sigma \frac{(O-E)^2}{E}$$

$$= \frac{(345-395.723)^2}{395.723} + \frac{(3614-3563.277)^2}{3563.277} + \frac{(101-50.277)^2}{50.277} + \frac{(402-452.723)^2}{452.723}$$

$$= 64.08 \quad \left[\chi^2_{.05(1)} = 3.84 \right]$$

Reject H_0.

6.31 Childhood delinquency in the Dabbs and Morris (1990) study.

a.

		Testosterone		
		High	Normal	Total
	No	366	3554	3920
		(391.824)	(3528.176)	
Delinquency	Yes	80	462	542
		(54.176)	(487.824)	
		446	4016	4462 = N

$$\chi^2 = \Sigma \frac{(O-E)^2}{E}$$

$$= \frac{(366-391.824)^2}{391.824} + \frac{(3554-3528.176)^2}{3528.176} + \frac{(80-54.176)^2}{54.176} + \frac{(462-487.824)^2}{487.824}$$

$$= 15.57 \quad \left[\chi^2_{.05(1)} = 3.84 \right]$$

Reject H_0.

b. There is a significant relationship between high levels of testosterone in adult men and a history of delinquent behavior during childhood.

c. This result shows that we can tie the two variables (delinquency and testosterone) together historically.

6.33   Good touch/Bad touch

a.

		Abused		
		Yes	No	Total
	Yes	43	457	500
Received		(56.85)	(443.15)	
Program	No	50	268	318
		(36.15)	(281.85)	
		93	725	$818 = N$

$$\chi^2 = \Sigma \frac{(O-E)^2}{E}$$
$$= \frac{(43-56.85)^2}{56.85} + \frac{(457-443.15)^2}{443.15} + ... + \frac{(268-281.85)^2}{281.85}$$
$$= 9.79 \qquad \left[\chi^2_{.05(1)} = 3.84\right]$$

Reject H_0.

b. Odds ratio

OR = (43/457)/(50/268) = 0.094/.186 = .505 Those who receive the program are about half as likely to subsequently suffer abuse.

6.35   Gender of parents and children.

a.

		Lost Parent Gender		
		Male	Female	Total
Child	Male	18	34	52
	Female	27	61	88
		45	95	$140 = N$

$$\chi^2 = .232 \, (p = .630)$$

b. There is no relationship between the gender of the lost parent and the gender of the child.

c. We would be unable to separate effects due to parental gender from effects due to the child's gender. They would be completely confounded.

6.37   We could ask a series of similar questions, evenly split between "right" and "wrong" answers. We could then sort the replies into positive and negative categories and ask whether faculty were more likely than students to give negative responses.

7.1 Distribution of 100 random numbers:

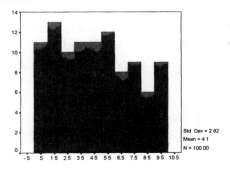

Number	Frequency
0	11
1	13
2	10
3	11
4	11
5	12
6	8
7	9
8	6
9	9

Descriptive Statistics

X	N	100
	Minimum	0
	Maximum	9
	Mean	4.10
	Std. Deviation	2.82
	N	100

7.3   Does the Central Limit Theorem work?

Population Parameters	Predictions from Central Limit Theorem	Empirical Sampling distribution
$\mu = 4.5$	$\bar{X} = 4.5$	$\bar{X} = 4.47$
$\sigma^2 = 6.76$	$s^2 = \dfrac{\sigma^2}{n} = \dfrac{6.76}{5} = 1.35$	$s^2 = 1.50$

The mean of the sampling distribution is very close to that predicted by the Central Limit theorem. The variance of the sampling distribution is a little high, but it is still approximately correct.

7.5   The standard error would have been smaller, because it would be estimated by $\sqrt{\dfrac{8.533}{15}}$ instead of $\sqrt{\dfrac{8.533}{5}}$.

7.7   First of all, these students scored better than we might have predicted, not worse. Second, these students are certainly not a random sample of high school students. Finally, there is no definition of what is meant by "a terrible state," nor any idea of whether or not the SAT measures such a concept.

7.9   This answer to Exercise 7.8 differs substantially from Exercise 7.6 because the sample sizes are so very different. I deliberately sought examples where the means were nearly the same, but with that large difference in sample size, so the resulting z values, and associated probabilities, are very different.

7.11   The Mean gain = 3.01, standard deviation = 7.31. $t = 2.22$. With 28 df the critical value = 2.048, so we will reject the null hypothesis and conclude that the girls gained at better than chance levels.

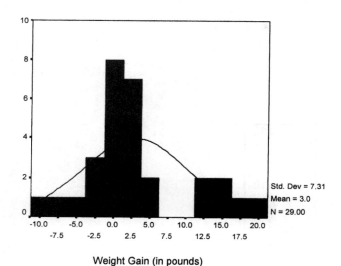

Weight Gain (in pounds)

7.13 **a.** Performance when not reading passage

$$t = \frac{\overline{X} - \mu}{s_{\overline{X}}} = \frac{\overline{X} - \mu}{\dfrac{s}{\sqrt{n}}}$$

$$= \frac{46.6 - 20.0}{\dfrac{6.8}{\sqrt{28}}} = \frac{26.6}{1.285} = 20.70$$

b. This does not mean that the SAT is not a valid measure, but it does show that people who do well at guessing at answers also do well on the SAT. This is not very surprising.

7.15 Confidence limits on μ for Exercise 7.14:

$$CI_{.95} = \overline{X} \pm t_{.05}\frac{s}{\sqrt{n}}$$

$$= 4.39 \pm 2.03\frac{2.61}{\sqrt{36}} = 4.39 \pm 0.883$$

$$= 3.507 \le \mu \le 5.273$$

An interval formed as this one was has a probability of .95 of encompassing the mean of the population. Since this interval includes the hypothesized population mean of 3.87, it is consistent with the results in Exercise 7.14.

7.17 We used a paired-t test in Exercise 7.16 because the data were paired in the sense of coming from the same subject. Some subjects showed generally more beta-endorphins at both times than others, and we wanted to eliminate this subject-to-subject variability that had nothing to do with stress. In fact, there isn't much of a relationship between the two measures, but we can't fairly ignore it after the fact.

7.19 Paired t test on marital satisfaction:

$$t = \frac{\overline{X}_1 - \overline{X}_2}{s_{\overline{X}_1 - \overline{X}_2}} = \frac{\overline{D}}{s_{\overline{D}}} = \frac{\overline{D}}{\dfrac{s_D}{\sqrt{n}}}$$

$$= \frac{2.725 - 2.791}{\dfrac{1.30}{\sqrt{91}}} = \frac{-.066}{.136} = -.485$$

We cannot reject the null hypothesis that males and females are equally satisfied. A paired-t is appropriate because it would not seem reasonable to assume that the sexual satisfaction of a husband is independent of that of his wife.

7.21 Correlation between husbands and wives:

$$r = \frac{\text{cov}_{XY}}{s_X s_Y} = \frac{0.420}{\sqrt{(1.357)(1.167)}} = \frac{0.420}{1.584} = \frac{.420}{1.259} = .334$$

The correlation between the scores of husbands and wives was .334, which is significant, and which confirms the assumption that the scores would be related.

7.23 The important question is what would the sampling distribution of the mean (or differences between means) look like, and with 91 pairs of scores that sampling distribution would be substantially continuous with a normal distribution of means.

7.25 Everitt's Family Therapy group:

a. We want to test the null hypothesis that the mean weight was the same before and after treatment.

$$t = \frac{\overline{X}_{After} - \overline{X}_{Before}}{s_{\overline{X}_{After} - \overline{X}_{Before}}} = \frac{\overline{D}}{s_{\overline{D}}} = \frac{\overline{D}}{\frac{s_D}{\sqrt{n}}}$$

$$= \frac{90.494 - 83.229}{\frac{7.157}{\sqrt{17}}} = \frac{7.265}{1.736} = 4.185$$

b. $t = 4.185$ on 16 *df*, which tells us that there was a significant gain in weight over the course of therapy.

7.27 Confidence limits on weight gain in Family Therapy group:

$$CI_{.95} = \overline{D} \pm t_{.025(16)} s_{\overline{D}}$$
$$= 7.265 \pm (2.12)(1.736) = 7.265 \pm 3.68$$

$$3.585 \leq \mu \leq 10.945$$

The probability is .95 that this procedure has resulted in limits that bracket the mean weight gain in the population.

7.29 **a.** Null hypothesis—there is not a significant difference in test scores between those who have read the passage and those who have not.

b. Alternative hypothesis—there is a significant difference between the two conditions.

c. $\quad t = \dfrac{\bar{X}_1 - \bar{X}_2}{\sqrt{\dfrac{s^2}{n_1} + \dfrac{s^2}{n_2}}}$ $\qquad$ where $\quad s^2 = \dfrac{(n_1 - 1)s_1^2 + (n_2 - 1)s_2^2}{n_1 + n_2 - 2}$

$$s^2 = \frac{16(10.6^2) + 27(6.8^2)}{17 + 28 - 2} = \frac{3046.24}{43} = 70.843$$

$$t = \frac{69.6 - 46.6}{\sqrt{\dfrac{70.843}{17} + \dfrac{70.843}{28}}} = \frac{23.0}{\sqrt{70.843\left(\dfrac{1}{17} + \dfrac{1}{28}\right)}} = \frac{23.0}{\sqrt{6.697}} = 8.89$$

$t = 8.89$ on 43 *df* if we pool the variances. This difference is significant.

d. We can conclude that students do better on this test if they read the passage on which they are going to answer questions.

7.31

$\quad t = \dfrac{\bar{X}_1 - \bar{X}_2}{\sqrt{\dfrac{s^2}{n_1} + \dfrac{s^2}{n_2}}}$ $\qquad$ where $\quad s^2 = \dfrac{(n_1 - 1)s_1^2 + (n_2 - 1)s_2^2}{n_1 + n_2 - 2}$

$$s^2 = \frac{25(63.82) + 16(51.23)}{26 + 17 - 2} = \frac{2415.18}{41} = 58.91$$

$$t = \frac{-0.45 - 7.26}{\sqrt{\dfrac{58.91}{26} + \dfrac{58.91}{17}}} = \frac{23.0}{\sqrt{58.91\left(\dfrac{1}{26} + \dfrac{1}{17}\right)}} = \frac{-7.71}{\sqrt{5.731}} = -3.22$$

A *t* on two independent groups = 3.22 on 41 *df*, which is significant. Family therapy led to significantly greater weight gain than the Control condition. (Variances were homogeneous.)

7.33 If those means had actually come from independent samples, we could not remove differences due to couples, and the resulting *t* would have been somewhat smaller.

7.35 The difference between the two answers in not greater than it is because the correlation between husbands and wives was actually quite low.

7.37 **a.** I would assume that the experimental hypothesis is the hypothesis that mothers of schizophrenic children provide TAT descriptions that show less positive parent-child relationships.

b. Normal   Mean = 3.55 $s = 1.887$ $n = 20$
Schizophrenic Mean = 2.10 $s = 1.553$ $n = 20$

$$t = \frac{\bar{X}_1 - \bar{X}_2}{\sqrt{\dfrac{s_1^2}{n_1} + \dfrac{s_2^2}{n_2}}} = \frac{3.55 - 2.10}{\sqrt{\dfrac{1.887^2}{20} + \dfrac{1.553^2}{20}}}$$

$$= \frac{1.45}{\sqrt{0.299}} = \frac{1.45}{0.546} = 2.66 \qquad \left[t_{.05(38)} = \pm 2.02 \right]$$

Reject the null hypothesis

This t is significant on 38 df, and I would conclude that the mean number of pictures portraying positive parent-child relationships is lower in the schizophrenic group than in the normal group.

7.39 There is no way to tell cause and effect relationships in Exercise 7.37. It could be that people who experience poor parent-child interaction are at risk for schizophrenia. But it could also be that schizophrenic children disrupt the family and poor relationships come as a result.

7.41 95% confidence limits

$$CI_{.05} = \left(\bar{X}_1 - \bar{X}_2 \right) \pm t_{.025} \sqrt{\frac{s^2}{n_1} + \frac{s^2}{n_2}}$$

$$= (18.778 - 17.625) \pm (2.131) \sqrt{\frac{16.362}{9} + \frac{16.362}{8}} = 1.153 \pm 4.189$$

$$-3.036 \leq \left(\mu_1 - \mu_2 \right) \leq 5.342$$

7.43   Repeating Exercise 7.42 with time as the dependent variable:

$$t = \frac{\bar{X}_1 - \bar{X}_2}{\sqrt{\dfrac{s_1^2}{n_1} + \dfrac{s_2^2}{n_2}}}$$

$$t = \frac{2.102 - 1.246}{\sqrt{\dfrac{0.714}{5} + \dfrac{0.091}{5}}} = \frac{0.856}{\sqrt{0.161}} = \frac{0.856}{0.401} = 2.134$$

The variances are very different, but even if we did not adjust the degrees of freedom, we would still fail to reject the null hypothesis.

7.45   If you take the absolute differences between the observations and their group means and run a t test comparing the two groups on the absolute differences, you obtain $t = 0.625$. Squaring this you have $F = 0.391$, which makes it clear that Levene's test in SPSS is operating on the absolute differences. (The t for squared differences would equal 0.213, which would give an F of 0.045.)

7.47 Differences between males and females on anxiety and depression:

(We cannot assume homogeneity of regression here.)

Independent Samples Test

Equal variances not assumed

	t-test for Equality of Means						
						95% Confidence Interval of the Difference	
	t	df	Sig. (2-tailed)	Mean Difference	Std. Error Difference	Lower	Upper
DEPRESST	3.256	248.346	.001	3.426	1.052	1.353	5.499
ANXT	1.670	246.260	.096	1.805	1.081	-.324	3.933

7.49   **a.** The scale of measurement is important because if we rescaled the categories as 1, 2, 4, and 6, for example, we would have quite different answers.

b. The first exercise asks if there is a relationship between the satisfaction of husbands and wives. The second simply asks if males (husbands) are more satisfied, on average, than females (wives).

c. You could adapt the suggestion made in the text about combining the t on independent groups and the t on matched groups.

d. I'm really not very comfortable with the t test because I am not pleased with the scale of measurement. An alternative would be a ranked test, but the number of ties is huge, and that probably worries me even more.

Chapter 8 - Power

8.1   Peer pressure study:

a.

$$d = \frac{\mu_1 - \mu_0}{\sigma}$$

$$= \frac{520 - 500}{80}$$

$$= .25$$

b. $f(n)$ for 1-sample t-test = $\sqrt{n}$

$$\delta = d\sqrt{n}$$

$$= .25\sqrt{100}$$

$$= 2.5$$

c.   Power = .71

8.3   Changing power in Exercise 8.1:

a.   For power = .70, $\delta = 2.475$

$$\delta = d\sqrt{n}$$

$$2.475 = .25\sqrt{n}$$

$$n = 98.01 \approx 99 \text{ (Round up, because students come in whole lots)}$$

b.   For power = .80, $\delta = 2.8$

$$\delta = d\sqrt{n}$$

$$2.8 = .25\sqrt{n}$$

$$n = 125.44 \approx 126 \text{(Round up)}$$

c.   For power = .90, $\delta = 3.25$

$$\delta = d\sqrt{n}$$

$$3.25 = .25\sqrt{n}$$

$$n = 169$$

8.5   Sampling distributions of the mean for the situation in Exercise 8.4:

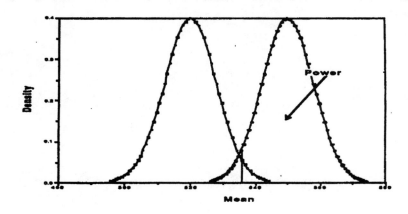

8.7   Avoidance behavior in rabbits using 1-sample t test:

a.

$$d = \frac{\mu_1 - \mu_0}{\delta} = \frac{5.8 - 4.8}{2} = \frac{1}{2} = .5$$

For power = .50, $\delta = 1.95$
$$\delta = d\sqrt{n}$$
$$1.95 = .5\sqrt{n}$$
$$n = 15.21 \approx 16$$

b. For power = .80, $\delta = 2.8$
$$\delta = d\sqrt{n}$$
$$2.8 = .5\sqrt{n}$$
$$n = 31.36 \approx 32$$

8.9   Avoidance behavior in rabbits with unequal ns:

$$d = .5$$
$$n = \overline{n}_h = \frac{2n_1 n_2}{n_1 + n_2}$$
$$= \frac{2(20)(15)}{20 + 15} = 17.14$$
$$\delta = d\sqrt{\frac{n}{2}} = 5\sqrt{\frac{17.14}{2}} = 1.46$$

power = .31

8.11   *t* test on data for Exercise 8.10

$$t = \frac{\overline{X}_1 - \overline{X}_2}{\sqrt{\dfrac{s_p^2}{n_1} + \dfrac{s_p^2}{n_2}}}$$

$$= \frac{25 - 30}{\sqrt{\dfrac{64}{20} + \dfrac{64}{20}}}$$

$$= -1.98$$

[$t_{.025(38)} = \pm 2.025$]   Do not reject the null hypothesis

c. *t* is numerically equal to δ although *t* is calculated from statistics and δ is calculated from parameters. In other words, δ = the *t* that you would get if the data exactly match what you think are the values of the parameters.

8.13   Diagram to defend answer to Exercise 8.12:

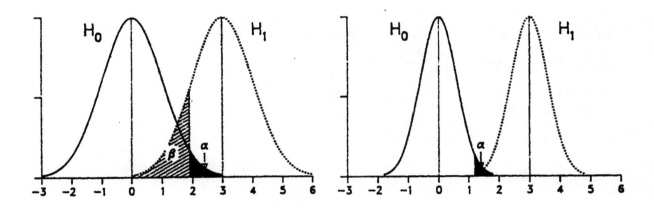

With larger sample sizes the sampling distribution of the mean has a smaller standard error, which means that there is less overlap of the distributions. This results in greater power, and therefore the larger *n*'s significant result was less impressive.

8.15 Social awareness of ex-delinquents--which subject pool would be better to use?

$$\bar{X}_{normal} = 38 \qquad n = 50$$

$$\bar{X}_{H.S.\ Grads} = 35 \qquad n = 100$$

$$\bar{X}_{dropout} = 30 \qquad n = 25$$

$$\mathbf{d} = \frac{38 - 35}{\sigma} \qquad\qquad \mathbf{d} = \frac{38 - 30}{\sigma}$$

$$\overline{N}_h = \frac{2(50)(100)}{150} = 66.67 \qquad \overline{N}_h = \frac{2(50)(25)}{75} = 33.33$$

$$\delta = \frac{3}{\sigma}\sqrt{\frac{66.67}{2}} = \frac{17.32}{\sigma} \qquad \delta = \frac{8}{\sigma}\sqrt{\frac{33.33}{2}} = \frac{32.66}{\sigma}$$

Assuming equal standard deviations, the H.S. dropout group of 25 would result in a higher value of δ and therefore higher power. (You can let σ be any value you choose, as long as it is the same for both calculations. Then calculate δ for each situation.)

8.17 Total sample sizes required for power = .60, α = .05, two-tailed (δ = 2.2):

Effect Size	d	One-sample t	Two-sample t Per Group	Overall
Small	0.2	120	242	484
Medium	0.5	20	39	78
Large	0.8	8	16	32

8.19 When can power = β?

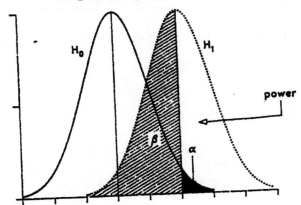

The mean under H_1 should fall at the critical value under H_0. The question implies a one-tailed test. Thus the mean is 1.645 standard errors above μ_0, which is 100.

$$\mu = 100 + 1.64\sigma_X$$
$$= 100 + 1.645\left(15/\sqrt{25}\right)$$
$$= 104.935$$

When $\mu = 104.935$, power would equal β.

8.21 Aronson's study:
a. The study would confound differences in lab that have nothing to do with the independent variable with the effect of that variable. You would not be able to draw sound conclusions unless you could persuade yourself that the labs were similar in all other relevant ways.

b. I would randomize the conditions across all of the students in the two labs combined.

c. The stereotypes do not apply to women, so I don't have any particular hypothesis about what would happen.

8.23 Questions of how to design a study properly are as much a part of statistics as questions about the proper sequence of steps to analyze the data.

Chapter 9 - Correlation and Regression

9.1   Scatter diagram of percentage of LBW infants (Y) and high-risk fertility rate (X_1) in Vermont Health Planning Districts.

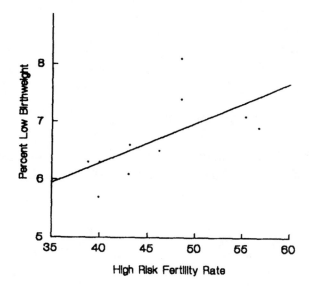

9.3   Correlation between percentage of LBW infants (Y) and percentage of births to unmarried mothers (X_2) in Vermont Health Planning Districts.

$$N = 10 \qquad\qquad s_Y = 0.698 \qquad\qquad s_{X_2} = 1.322 \qquad \mathrm{cov}_{X_2 Y} = 0.3189$$

$$r = \frac{\mathrm{cov}_{X_2 Y}}{s_{X_2} s_Y} = \frac{0.3189}{(1.322(0.698)} = .35$$

9.5   Three sets of data:

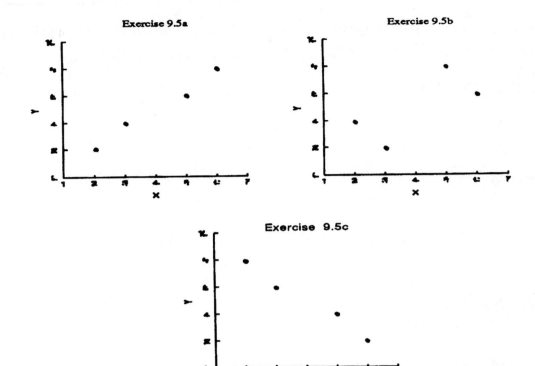

9.7   Correlations for the three data sets in Exercise 9.5:

a.

$$r = \frac{cov_{XY}}{s_X s_Y}$$ For each set, $s_X = 1.826$ and $s_Y = 2.582$

Set 1:
$$r = \frac{cov_{XY}}{s_X s_Y} = \frac{4.67}{(1.826)(2.582)} = .99$$

Set 2:
$$r = \frac{cov_{XY}}{s_X s_Y} = \frac{3.33}{(1.826)(2.582)} = .71$$

Set 3:
$$r = \frac{cov_{XY}}{s_X s_Y} = \frac{-4.67}{(1.826)(2.582)} = -.99$$

b. Three arrangements of Y will result in the lowest possible positive correlation:

2 8 6 4   or   6 4 2 8   or   6 2 8 4   [$r = .14$]

9.9   Cerebral hemorrhage in low-birthweight infants and cognitive deficit at age 5:

a. Power calculation:

$\mathbf{d} = .20$

$\delta = \mathbf{d}\sqrt{N-1}$

$\quad = .20\sqrt{25-1}$

$\quad = 0.980 \quad \text{power} = .17$

b. For power $= .80, \delta = 2.8$

$\delta = \mathbf{d}\sqrt{N-1}$

$2.8 = .20\sqrt{N-1}$

$N = 197$

9.11   Standard error of estimate for regression equation in Exercise 9.10:

$N = 10 \qquad r = .62$ [Calculated in Exercise 9.2]

$s_{Y.X} = s_Y\sqrt{\left(1-r^2\right)\dfrac{N-1}{N-2}} = .698\sqrt{\left(1-.62^2\right)(9/8)} = .580$

9.13   If high-risk fertility rate in Exercise 9.10 jumped to 70:

$\hat{Y} = bX + a$

$\quad = .069(70) + 3.53$

$\quad = 8.36$ would be the predicted percentage of LBW infants born.

9.15   Number of symptoms predicted for a stress score of 8 using the data in Table 9.3 :

Regression equation: $\hat{Y} = 0.7831(X) + 73.891$

If Stress score (X) = 8: $\hat{Y} = 0.7831(8) + 73.891$

Predicted Number of symptoms: $\hat{Y} = 80.156$

9.17 Confidence interval on $\hat{Y}$

$$CI(Y) = \hat{Y} \pm t_{\alpha/2}\left(s'_{Y.X}\right)$$

$$s'_{Y.X} = s_{Y.X}\sqrt{1 + \frac{1}{N} + \frac{(X_i - \overline{X})^2}{(N-1)s_X^2}} = 17.563\sqrt{1 + \frac{1}{107} + \frac{(X_i - \overline{X})^2}{106(171.505)}}$$

$$\hat{Y} = 0.7831X + 73.891$$
$$t_{\alpha/2} = 1.984$$

For several different values of X, calculate $\hat{Y}$ and s'$_{Y.X}$ and plot the results.

9.19 When data are standardized, the slope equals r. Therefore the slope will be less than one for all but the most trivial case, and predicted deviations from the mean will be less than actual parental deviations.

9.21 Number of subjects needed in Exercise 9.20 for power = .80:

For power = .80, $\delta = 2.80$

$$\delta = \rho_1\sqrt{N-1}$$
$$2.80 = .40\sqrt{30-1}$$
$$N = 50$$

9.23 Katz et al. correlations with SAT scores.

a. $r_1 = .68$ $r_1' = .829$

$r_2 = .51$ $r_2' = .563$

$$z = \frac{r_1' - r_2'}{\sqrt{\dfrac{1}{N_1 - 3} + \dfrac{1}{N_2 - 3}}} = \frac{.829 - .563}{\sqrt{\dfrac{1}{14} + \dfrac{1}{25}}} = 0.797$$

The correlations are not significantly different from each other.

b. We do not have reason to argue that the relationship between performance and prior test scores is affected by whether or not the student read the passage.

9.25   It is difficult to tell whether the significant difference between the results of the two previous problems is to be attributable to the larger sample sizes or the higher (and thus more different) values of r'. It is likely to be the former.

9.27   Moore and McCabe example of alcohol and tobacco use:

Correlations

		ALCOHOL	TOBACCO
ALCOHOL	Pearson Correlation	1.000	.224
	Sig. (2-tailed)	.	.509
	N	11	11
TOBACCO	Pearson Correlation	.224	1.000
	Sig. (2-tailed)	.509	.
	N	11	11

b. The data suggest that people from Northern Ireland actually drink relatively little.

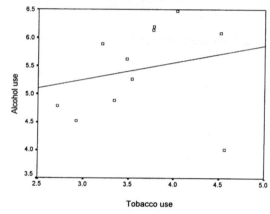

c. With Northern Ireland excluded from the data the correlation is .784, which is significant at $p = .007$.

9.29   **a.** The correlations range between .40 and .80.

b. The subscales are not measuring independent aspects of psychological well-being.

44

9.31   Relationship between height and weight for males:

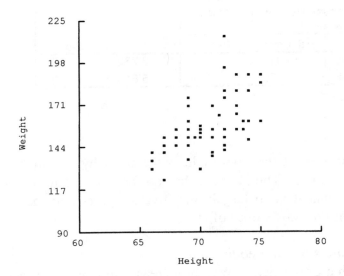

Scatterplot for Males

The regression solution that follows was produced by SPSS and gives all relevant results.

Model Summary[b]

Model	R	R Square	Adjusted R Square	Std. Error of the Estimate
1	.604[a]	.364	.353	14.9917

a. Predictors: (Constant), HEIGHT

b. Gender = Male

ANOVA[b,c]

Model		Sum of Squares	df	Mean Square	F	Sig.
1	Regression	7087.800	1	7087.800	31.536	.000[a]
	Residual	12361.253	55	224.750		
	Total	19449.053	56			

a. Predictors: (Constant), HEIGHT

b. Dependent Variable: WEIGHT

c. Gender = Male

45

Coefficients[a,b]

Model		Unstandardized Coefficients		Standardized Coefficients	t	Sig.
		B	Std. Error	Beta		
1	(Constant)	-149.934	54.917		-2.730	.008
	HEIGHT	4.356	.776	.604	5.616	.000

a. Dependent Variable: WEIGHT

b. Gender = Male

With a slope of 4.36, the data predict that two males who differ by one inch will also differ by approximately 4 1/3 pounds. The intercept has no meaning because people are not 0 inches tall, but the fact that it is so largely negative suggests that there is some curvilinearity in this relationship for low values of Height.

Tests on the correlation and the slope are equivalent tests when we have one predictor, and these tests tell us that both are significant. Weight increases reliably with increases in height.

9.33   As a 5'8" male, my predicted weight is $\hat{Y}$ = 4.356(Height) - 149.934 = 4.356*68 - 149.934 = 146.27 pounds.

a. I weigh 146 pounds. (Well, I did two years ago.) Therefore the residual in the prediction is $Y - \hat{Y}$ = 146 - 146.27 = -0.27.

b. If the students on which this equation is based under- or over-estimated their own height or weight, the prediction for my weight will be based on invalid data and will be systematically in error.

9.35   The male would be predicted to weigh 137.562 pounds, while the female would be predicted to weigh 125.354 pounds. The predicted difference between them would be 12.712 pounds.

9.37   Independence of trials in reaction time study.

The data were plotted by "trial", where a larger trial number represents an observation later in the sequence.

46

RxTime as a Function of Trials

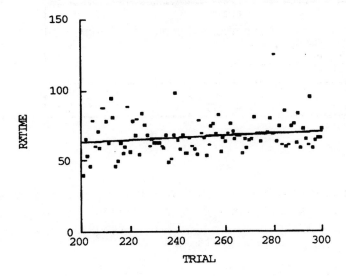

Although the regression line has a slight positive slope, the slope is not significantly different from zero. This is shown below.

```
DEP VAR:   TRIAL        N:      100   MULTIPLE R: 0.181   SQUARED MULTIPLE R: 0.033
ADJUSTED SQUARED MULTIPLE R:  0.023     STANDARD ERROR OF ESTIMATE:     28.67506


VARIABLE        COEFFICIENT     STD ERROR     STD COEF TOLERANCE      T    P(2 TAIL)


CONSTANT          221.84259     15.94843      0.00000     .        .14E+02  .10E-14
RXTIME              0.42862      0.23465      0.18146  1.00000    1.82665   0.07080

                        ANALYSIS OF VARIANCE
SOURCE          SUM-OF-SQUARES   DF   MEAN-SQUARE      F-RATIO        P


REGRESSION        2743.58452     1    2743.58452      3.33664      0.07080
RESIDUAL         80581.41548    98     822.25934
```

There is not a systematic linear or cyclical trend over time, and we would probably be safe in assuming that the observations can be treated as if they were independent. Any slight dependency would not alter our results to a meaningful degree.

Chapter 10 - Alternative Correlational Techniques

10.1   Performance ratings in the morning related to perceived peak time of day:

    a.   Plot of data with regression line:

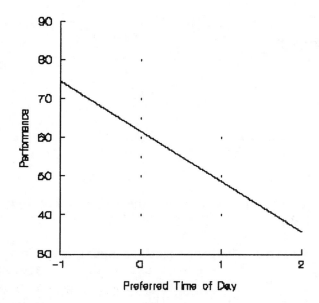

    b.

$$s_X = 0.489$$

$$s_Y = 11.743$$

$$cov_{XY} = -3.105$$

$$r_{pb} = \frac{cov_{XY}}{s_X s_Y} = \frac{-3.105}{(0.489)(11.743)} = -.540$$

$$t = \frac{r\sqrt{(N-2)}}{\sqrt{1-r^2}} = \frac{(-.540)\sqrt{18}}{\sqrt{.708}} = \frac{-2.291}{.842} = -2.723 \quad [p < .01]$$

    c.   Performance in the morning is significantly related to people's perceptions of their peak periods.

10.3   It looks as if morning people vary their performance across time, but that evening people are uniformly poor.

10.5 Running a t test on the data in Exercise 10.1:

$\bar{X}_1 = 61.538$ $\qquad$ $s_1^2 = 114.103$ $\qquad$ $n_1 = 13$

$\bar{X}_2 = 48.571$ $\qquad$ $s_2^2 = 80.952$ $\qquad$ $n_2 = 7$

$$s_p^2 = \frac{(n_1-1)s_1^2 + (n_2-1)s_2^2}{n_1+n_2-2} = \frac{(13-1)114.103+(7-1)80.952}{13+7-2} = 103.053$$

$$t = \frac{\bar{X}_1 - \bar{X}_2}{\sqrt{s_p^2\left(\frac{1}{n_1}+\frac{1}{n_2}\right)}} = \frac{61.538-48.571}{\sqrt{103.053\left(\frac{1}{13}+\frac{1}{7}\right)}} = 2.725$$

$[t_{.025(18)} = \pm 2.101]$ $\qquad\qquad$ Reject H_0

The t calculated here (2.725) is equal to the t calculated to test the significance of the r calculated in Exercise 10.1.

10.7 Regression equation for relationship between college GPA and completion of Ph.D. program:

$$b = \frac{\text{cov}_{XY}}{s_X^2} = \frac{0.051}{.503^2} = .202$$

$$a = \frac{\Sigma Y - b\Sigma X}{N} = \frac{17 - .202(72.58)}{25} = .093$$

$\hat{Y} = bX + a = .202X + .093$

When $X = \bar{X} = 2.9032$, $\hat{Y} = .202(2.9032) + .093 = .680 = \bar{Y}$.

10.9 Establishment of a GPA cutoff of 3.00:

a. Ph.D. (Y):

0	0	0	0	0	0	0	0	1	1
1	1	1	1	1	1	1	1	1	1
1	1	1							

GPA (X):	0	1	0	1	1	0	0	0	1	0
	1	1	1	1	0	1	1	1	0	0	0	1
	1	1	0							

b.

$$s_X = 0.507$$

$$s_Y = 0.476$$

$$\text{cov}_{XY} = 0.062$$

$$\phi = \frac{0.062}{(0.507)(0.476)} = .256$$

c.
$$t = \frac{r\sqrt{(N-2)}}{\sqrt{1-r^2}} = \frac{(.256)\sqrt{23}}{\sqrt{.934}} = \frac{1.228}{.967} = 1.27 \quad \text{[not significant]}$$

10.11 Alcoholism and childhood history of ADD:

a.

$$s_X = 0.471$$

$$s_Y = 0.457$$

$$\text{cov}_{XY} = 0.135$$

$$\phi = \frac{0.135}{(0.471)(0.457)} = .628$$

b. $\quad \chi^2 = N\phi^2 = 32(.628^2) = 12.62 \quad [p < .05]$

10.13 Development ordering of language skills using Kendall's τ

a.

$$\tau = 1 - \frac{2(\# \text{ inversions})}{\# \text{ pairs}} = 1 - \frac{2(6)}{15(14)/2} = 1 - \frac{23}{105} = .886$$

b.

$$z = \frac{\tau}{\sqrt{\dfrac{2(2N+5)}{9N(N-1)}}} = \frac{.886}{\sqrt{\dfrac{2(30+5)}{9(15)(14)}}} = \frac{.886}{\sqrt{.037}} = 4.60 \quad [p < .05]$$

10.15 Ranking of videotapes of children's behaviors by clinical graduate students and experienced clinicians using Kendall's τ:

```
Exp.      New
1         2
2         1
3         4
4         3
5         5
6         8
7         6
8        10
9         7
10        9
```

$$\tau = 1 - \frac{2(\# \text{ inversions})}{\# \text{ pairs}} = 1 = \frac{2(6)}{10(9)/2} = 1 - \frac{12}{45} = .733$$

10.17 Verification of Rosenthal and Rubin's statement

	Improvement	No Improvement	Total
Therapy	66	34	100
	(50)	(50)	
No Therapy	34	66	100
	(50)	(50)	
Total	100	100	200

a.

$$\chi^2 = \Sigma \frac{(O-E)^2}{E} = \frac{(66-50)^2}{50} + \frac{(34-50)^2}{50} + \frac{(34-50)^2}{50} + \frac{(66-50)^2}{50}$$

$$= 20.48$$

b. An $r^2 = .0512$ would correspond to $\chi^2 = 10.24$. The closest that you can come to this result is if the subjects were split 61/39 in the first condition and 39/61 in the second (rounding to integers.)

10.19 ClinCase against Group in Mireault's data

	ClinCase	
	0	1
Loss	69	66
Married	108	73
Divorced	36	23

a. $\chi^2 = 2.815$ $[p = .245]$
$\phi_C = .087$

c. This approach would be preferred over the approach used in Chapter 7 if you had reason to believe that differences in depression scores below the clinical cutoff were of no importance and should be ignored.

10.21 **b.** If a statistic is not significant, that means that we have no reason to believe that it is reliably different from 0 (or whatever the parameter under H_0). In the case of a correlation, if it is not significant, that means that we have no reason to believe that there is a relationship between the two variables. Therefore it cannot be important.

c. With the exceptions of issues of power, sample size will not make an effect more important than it is. Increasing N will increase our level of significance, but the magnitude of the effect will be unaffected.

Chapter 11 - Simple Analysis of Variance

11.1 Retrieval of rat pups:

Descriptives

TIME

	N	Mean	Std. Deviation	Std. Error
5 days	6	17.1667	5.1153	2.0883
20 days	6	22.1667	5.1153	2.0883
35 days	6	42.1667	5.1153	2.0883
Total	18	27.1667	12.1086	2.8540

$$SS_{total} = \Sigma \left(X_{ij} - \bar{X}_{..} \right)^2 = (15 - 27.1667)^2 +$$
$$(10 - 27.1667)^2 + \ldots + (40 - 27.1667)^2$$
$$= 2492.5$$

$$SS_{treat} = n\Sigma \left(\bar{X}_J - \bar{X}_{..} \right)^2 = 6\left((17.1667 - 27.1667)^2 + (22.1667 - 27.1667)^2 + (42.1667 - 27.1667)^2 \right)$$
$$= 6(350.00) = 2100$$

$$SS_{error} = SS_{total} - SS_{treat} = 2492.50 - 2100.00 = 392.50$$

ANOVA

TIME

	Sum of Squares	df	Mean Square	F	Sig.
Between Groups	2100.000	2	1050.000	40.127	.000
Within Groups	392.500	15	26.167		
Total	2492.500	17			

11.3   Recall in Eysenck (1974) for four Age/Levels of Processing groups:

Descriptives

RECALL

	N	Mean	Std. Deviation	Std. Error
1.00	10	6.5000	1.4337	.4534
2.00	10	19.3000	2.6687	.8439
3.00	10	7.0000	1.8257	.5774
4.00	10	12.0000	3.7417	1.1832
Total	40	11.2000	5.7699	.9123

a.

$$SS_{total} = \Sigma \left(X_{ij} - \bar{X}_{..} \right)^2 = \left(8 - 11.2\right)^2 + \left(6 - 11.2\right)^2 + ... + \left(11 - 11.2\right)^2$$
$$= 1298.4$$

$$SS_{treat} = n\Sigma \left(\bar{X}_j - \bar{X}_{..} \right)^2 = 10 \left(\begin{array}{c} \left(6.5 - 11.2\right)^2 + \left(19.3 - 11.2\right)^2 + \\ \left(7.0 - 11.2\right)^2 + \left(12.0 - 11.2\right)^2 \end{array} \right)$$
$$= 10\left(105.98\right) = 1059.8$$

$$SS_{error} = SS_{total} - SS_{treat} = 1298.4 - 1059.8 = 238.6$$

ANOVA

RECALL

	Sum of Squares	df	Mean Square	F	Sig.
Between Groups	1059.800	3	353.267	53.301	.000
Within Groups	238.600	36	6.628		
Total	1298.400	39			

b.   Groups 1 and 3 combined versus 2 and 4 combined:

Descriptives

RECALL

	N	Mean	Std. Deviation	Std. Error
Low	20	6.7500	1.6182	.3618
High	20	15.6500	4.9019	1.0961
Total	40	11.2000	5.7699	.9123

$$SS_{total} = \Sigma \left(X_{ij} - \bar{X}_{..} \right)^2 = (8 - 11.20)^2 + (6 - 11.20)^2 + ... + (11 - 11.20)^2$$
$$= 1298.40$$

$$SS_{treat} = n\Sigma \left(\bar{X}_{J} - \bar{X}_{..} \right)^2 = 20\left((6.75 - 11.20)^2 + (15.65 - 11.20)^2 \right)$$
$$= 20(39.605) = 792.1$$

$$SS_{error} = SS_{total} - SS_{treat} = 1298.4 - 792.1 = 502.3$$

ANOVA

RECALL

	Sum of Squares	df	Mean Square	F	Sig.
Between Groups	792.100	1	792.100	59.451	.000
Within Groups	506.300	38	13.324		
Total	1298.400	39			

c. The results are somewhat difficult to interpret because the error term now includes variance between younger and older participants. Notice that this is roughly double what it was in part a. In addition, we do not know whether the level of processing effect is true for both age groups, or if it applies primarily to one group.

11.5 Rerun of Exercise 11.2 with additional subjects:

The following is abbreviated printout from SPSS

a.

Descriptives [a]

RECALL

	N	Mean	Std. Deviation	Std. Error
Younger	12	18.4167	3.2039	.9249
Older	10	12.0000	3.7417	1.1832
Total	22	15.5000	4.6980	1.0016

a. PROCESS = High

ANOVA[a]

RECALL

	Sum of Squares	df	Mean Square	F	Sig.
Between Groups	224.583	1	224.583	18.800	.000
Within Groups	238.917	20	11.946		
Total	463.500	21			

a. PROCESS = High

b. and c. With and without pooling variances:

Independent Samples Test [a]

		t-test for Equality of Means				
		t	df	Sig. (2-tailed)	Mean Difference	Std. Error Difference
RECALL	Equal variances assumed	4.336	20	.000	6.4167	1.4799
	Equal variances not assumed	4.273	17.893	.000	6.4167	1.5018

a PROCESS = High

d. The squared t for the pooled case = $4.3359^2 = 18.80$, which is the F in the analysis of variance.

11.7   Magnitude of effect measures for Exercise 11.3a:

$$\eta^2 = \frac{SS_{group}}{SS_{total}} = \frac{1059.8}{1298.4} = .82$$

$$\omega^2 = \frac{SS_{group} - (k-1)MS_{error}}{SS_{total} + MS_{error}} = \frac{1059.8 - (4-1)6.63}{1298.4 + 6.63} = .80$$

11.9   Magnitude of effect for Foa et al. (1991) study:

$$\eta^2 = \frac{SS_{group}}{SS_{total}} = \frac{507.840}{2786.907} = .18$$

$$\omega^2 = \frac{SS_{group} - (k-1)MS_{error}}{SS_{total} + MS_{error}} = \frac{507.840 - (4-1)55.587}{2786.907 + 55.587} = .12$$

11.11   The results are basically the same as ours, although we are presented with confidence limits on group means and r^2 (which is really η^2).

11.13   Model for Exercise 11.1:

$X_{ij} = \mu + \tau_j + e_{ij}$
where
   μ = grand mean
   τ_j = the effect of the jth treatment
   e_{ij} = the unit of error for the ith subject in treatment$_j$

11.15   Model for Exercise 11.3:

$X_{ij} = \mu + \tau_j + e_{ij}$
where
   μ = grand mean
   τ_j = the effect of the jth treatment (where a "treatment" is a particular combination of Age and Task.
   e_{ij} = the unit of error for the ith subject in treatment j

11.17 Howell & Huessy (1981) study of ADD in elementary school vs. GPA in high school:

Group	Group Means	s_j^2	n_j
Never ADD	2.6774	0.9450	201
2nd only	1.6123	1.0195	13
4th only	1.9975	0.5840	12
2nd & 4th	2.0287	0.2982	8
5th only	1.7000	0.7723	14
2nd & 5th	1.9000	1.0646	9
4th & 5th	1.8986	0.0927	7
all 3 yrs	1.4225	0.3462	8
Overall	2.4444		272

$$SS_{group} = \Sigma n_j \left(\bar{X}_j - \bar{X}_{..} \right)^2$$
$$= 201(2.6774 - 2.4444)^2 + 13(1.6123 - 2.4444)^2 + ... + 8(1.4225 - 2.4444)^2$$
$$= 44.5570$$

$MS_{error.}$ = average variance (weighted)
$$= \frac{200 * 0.9450 + 12 * 1.0195 + ... + 7 * 0.3462}{200 + 12 + ... + 7} = 0.8761$$

ANOVA

GPA

	Sum of Squares	df	Mean Square	F	Sig.
Between Groups	44.557	7	6.365	7.266	.000
Within Groups	231.282	264	.876		
Total	275.839	271			

11.19 Square Root Transformation of data in Table 11.5:

Original data:	Control	0.1	0.5	1	2
	130	93	510	229	144
	94	444	416	475	111
	225	403	154	348	217
	105	192	636	276	200
	92	67	396	167	84
	190	170	451	151	99
	32	77	376	107	44
	64	353	192	235	84
	69	365	384		284
	93	422			293
Means	109.4	258.6	390.56	248.5	156
S.D.	58.5	153.32	147.68	118.74	87.65
Var	3421.82	23506.04	21809.78	14098.86	7682.22
n	10	10	9	8	10

Square root transformed data:

	Control	0.1	0.5	1	2
	11.402	9.644	22.583	15.133	12.000
	9.695	21.071	20.396	21.794	10.536
	15.000	20.075	12.410	18.655	14.731
	10.247	13.856	25.219	16.613	14.142
	9.592	8.185	19.900	12.923	9.165
	13.784	13.038	21.237	12.288	9.950
	5.657	8.775	19.391	10.344	6.633
	8.000	18.788	13.856	15.330	9.165
	8.307	19.105	19.596		16.852
	9.644	20.543			17.117
Means	10.13	15.31	19.40	15.39	12.03
S.D.	2.73	5.19	4.00	3.67	3.54
Var	7.48	26.96	16.03	13.49	12.55
n	10	10	9	8	10	47=N

11.21 Magnitude of effect for data in Exercise 11.17:

$$\eta^2 = \frac{SS_{group}}{SS_{total}} \qquad\qquad \omega^2 = \frac{SS_{group} - (K-1)MS_{error}}{SS_{total} + MS_{error}}$$

$$= \frac{44.557}{275.839} = .16 \qquad\qquad = \frac{44.557 - (8-1)0.876}{275.839 + 0.876} = .1389$$

11.23 Transforming Time to Speed in Exercise 11.22 involves a reciprocal transformation. The effect of the transformation is to decrease the relative distance between large values.

11.25 The parts of speech (noun vs. verb) are fixed. But the individual items within those parts of speech may well be random, representing a random sample of nouns and a random sample of verbs.

11.27 Computer exercise. Reanalysis of data from Exercise 7.46. The following is SPSS printout.

Descriptives

GSIT

	N	Mean	Std. Deviation	Std. Error
1	135	62.474	9.553	.822
2	181	62.199	8.522	.633
3	59	60.593	10.577	1.377
Total	375	62.045	9.242	.477

ANOVA

GSIT

	Sum of Squares	df	Mean Square	F	Sig.
Between Groups	153.493	2	76.747	.898	.408
Within Groups	31790.736	372	85.459		
Total	31944.229	374			

11.29 Computer exercise. Analysis of Epinuneq.dat from Introini-Collison and McGaugh (1986). These results come from SPSS.

INTERVAL = 1

Descriptives [a]

ERRORS

	N	Mean	Std. Deviation	Std. Error
1	18	3.33	1.78	.42
2	18	5.33	.97	.23
3	18	1.83	1.47	.35
Total	54	3.50	2.03	.28

a. INTERVAL = 1

ANOVA[a]

ERRORS

	Sum of Squares	df	Mean Square	F	Sig.
Between Groups	111.000	2	55.500	26.577	.000
Within Groups	106.500	51	2.088		
Total	217.500	53			

a. INTERVAL = 1

INTERVAL = 2

Descriptives [a]

ERRORS

	N	Mean	Std. Deviation	Std. Error
1	12	2.83	1.27	.37
2	12	4.42	1.38	.40
3	12	2.17	1.40	.41
Total	36	3.14	1.62	.27

a. INTERVAL = 2

ANOVA[a]

ERRORS

	Sum of Squares	df	Mean Square	F	Sig.
Between Groups	32.056	2	16.028	8.779	.001
Within Groups	60.250	33	1.826		
Total	92.306	35			

a. INTERVAL = 2

INTERVAL = 3

Descriptives [a]

ERRORS

	N	Mean	Std. Deviation	Std. Error
1	12	3.17	1.40	.41
2	12	4.42	1.31	.38
3	6	2.33	1.63	.67
Total	30	3.50	1.59	.29

a. INTERVAL = 3

ANOVA[a]

ERRORS

	Sum of Squares	df	Mean Square	F	Sig.
Between Groups	19.583	2	9.792	4.903	.015
Within Groups	53.917	27	1.997		
Total	73.500	29			

a. INTERVAL = 3

$F = 0.56$. There are no differences in the number of errors across the three Intervals.

11.31 I am trying to get students to commit themselves to the idea that transformations are not outlandish things to do to data.

11.33 You need to see that the pattern of differences among means is important in terms of the overall F.

Chapter 12 Multiple Comparisons Among Treatment Means

12.1 The effects of food and water deprivation on a learning task:

a. ANOVA with linear contrasts:

Groups	ad lib (1)	2/day (2)	food (3)	water (4)	f & w (5)	
Means:	18	24	8	12	11	
a_j:	3	3	-2	-2	-2	$30 = \Sigma a_j^2$
b_j:	1	-1	0	0	0	$2 = \Sigma b_j^2$
c_j:	0	0	1	1	-2	$6 = \Sigma c_j^2$
d_j:	0	0	1	-1	0	$2 = \Sigma d_j^2$

$$L_1 = \Sigma a_j \overline{X}_j = (3)(18) + (3)(24) + (-2)(8) + (-2)(12) + (-2)(11) = 64$$

$$L_2 = \Sigma b_j \overline{X}_j = (1)(18) + (-1)(24) + (0)(8) + (0)(12) + (0)(11) = -6$$

$$L_3 = \Sigma c_j \overline{X}_j = (0)(18) + (0)(24) + (1)(8) + (1)(12) + (-2)(11) = -2$$

$$L_4 = \Sigma d_j \overline{X}_j = (0)(18) + (0)(24) + (1)(8) + (-1)(12) + (0)(11) = -4$$

$$SS_{contrast_1} = \frac{nL^2}{\Sigma a_j^2} = \frac{5(64)^2}{30} = 862.667 \qquad SS_{contrast_3} = \frac{nL^2}{\Sigma c_j^2} = \frac{5(-2)^2}{6} = 3.333$$

$$SS_{contrast_2} = \frac{nL^2}{\Sigma b_j^2} = \frac{5(-6)^2}{2} = 90.000 \qquad SS_{contrast_4} = \frac{nL^2}{\Sigma d_j^2} = \frac{5(-4)^2}{2} = 40.000$$

Source	df	SS	MS	F
Deprivation	4	816.000	204.000	36.429*
1&2 vs 3,4,5	1	682.667	682.667	121.905*
1 vs 2	1	90.000	90.000	16.071*
3&4 vs 5	1	3.333	3.333	<1
3 vs 4	1	40.000	40.000	7.143*
Error	20	112.000	5.600	
Total	24	928.000		

$*p < .05 \quad [F_{.05(4,20)} = 2.87; F_{.05(1,20)} = 4.35]$

b. Orthogonality of contrasts:

Cross-products of coefficients:

$$\Sigma a_j b_j = (3)(1) + (3)(-1) + (-2)(0) + (-2)(0) + (-2)(0) = 0$$
$$\Sigma a_j c_j = (3)(0) + (3)(0) + (-2)(1) + (-2)(1) + (-2)(-2) = 0$$
$$\Sigma a_j d_j = (3)(0) + (3)(0) + (-2)(1) + (-2)(-1) + (-2)(0) = 0$$
$$\Sigma b_j c_j = (1)(0) + (-1)(0) + (0)(1) + (0)(1) + (0)(-2) = 0$$
$$\Sigma c_j d_j = (0)(0) + (0)(0) + (1)(1) + (1)(-1) + (-2)(0) = 0$$

c.

$$SS_{treat} = \Sigma SS_{contrast}$$
$$816.000 = 682.667 + 90.000 + 3.333 + 40.000$$

12.3 For $\alpha = .05$:

Per comparison error rate $= \alpha = .05$
Familywise error rate $= 1 - (1 - \alpha)^2 = .0975$.

12.5 Studentized range statistic for data in Exercise 11.2:

$$\overline{X}_1 = 19.3 \quad n_1 = 10$$
$$\overline{X}_2 = 12.0 \quad n_2 = 10$$

$$q_2 = \frac{\overline{X}_1 - \overline{X}_2}{\sqrt{\dfrac{MS_{error}}{n}}} = \frac{19.3 - 12.0}{\sqrt{\dfrac{10.56}{10}}} = \frac{7.3}{1.028} = 7.101$$

$$q_2 = 7.10 = 5.023 \sqrt{2} = 7.10 = t\sqrt{2}$$

12.7 The Bonferroni test on contrasts in Exercise 12.2 (data from Exercise 11.1):

From Exercise 12.2: $L_1 = -30.00$ $L_2 = -20.00$ $n = 6$

$\Sigma a_j^2 = 6$ $\Sigma b_j^2 = 2$ $MS_{error} = 26.167$

$$t' = \frac{L}{\sqrt{\dfrac{\Sigma a_j^2 MS_{error}}{n}}}$$

$$t_1' = \frac{-30.00}{\sqrt{\dfrac{6(26.167)}{6}}} = -5.86 \qquad t_2' = \frac{-20.00}{\sqrt{\dfrac{2(26.167)}{6}}} = -6.77$$

$$[t_{.05}\left(df_{error} = 15; 2 \text{ comparisons}\right) = 2.49) \qquad \text{Reject } H_0 \text{ in each case.}$$

12.9 Holm's multistage test for data in Exercise 12.1.

Comparison	F	t	c	$t_{.05(20,c)}$	Signif
1&2 vs 3,4,5	121.905	11.04	4	2.74	*
1 vs. 2	16.071	4.01	3	2.61	*
3 vs. 4	7.143	2.67	2	2.42	*
3&4 vs. 5	<1	<1	1	2.09	

Reject the first three null hypotheses but not the fourth. If this had been a standard Bonferroni test we would have rejected only the first two null hypotheses.

12.11 Tukey's test on example in Table 11.2:

Tukey's test is the same as the Newman-Keuls test except that the first (most conservative) q_r is taken as the critical value for all comparisons, and denoted q_{HSD}.

Group	Rhyme	Count	Adj	Intent	Image	r	q_{HSD}	W_r
Means	6.9	7.0	11	12	13.4			
Rhyme	--	0.1	4.1	5.1	6.5	5	4.04	3.973
Count		--	4.0	5.0	6.4	4	4.04	3.973
Adj			--	1.0	2.4	3	4.04	3.973
Intent				--	1.4	2	4.04	3.973
Image					--			

Significance Group:	Rhyme	Count	Adj	Intent	Image
Means:	6.9	7.0	11.0	12.0	13.4
Rhyme			*	*	*
Count			*	*	*
Adj					
Intent					
Image					

The counting and imagery groups are homogeneous, but are different from the adjective, intentional, and rhyming conditions, which are also homogeneous. This is the same pattern of differences that we found with the Newman-Keuls.

For the Tukey test SPSS produces the same table as we saw with the Newman-Keuls, but it also produces the following table, which contains the same information.

Multiple Comparisons

Dependent Variable: RECALL

Tukey HSD

(I) CONDTION	(J) CONDTION	Mean Difference (I-J)	Std. Error	Sig.	95% Confidence Interval	
					Lower Bound	Upper Bound
Counting	Rhyming	1.00E-01	1.39	1.000	-3.85	4.05
	Adjective	-4.00*	1.39	.046	-7.95	-4.77E-02
	Imagery	-6.40*	1.39	.000	-10.35	-2.45
	Intentional	-5.00*	1.39	.007	-8.95	-1.05
Rhyming	Counting	-1.00E-01	1.39	1.000	-4.05	3.85
	Adjective	-4.10*	1.39	.039	-8.05	-.15
	Imagery	-6.50*	1.39	.000	-10.45	-2.55
	Intentional	-5.10*	1.39	.006	-9.05	-1.15
Adjective	Counting	4.00*	1.39	.046	4.77E-02	7.95
	Rhyming	4.10*	1.39	.039	.15	8.05
	Imagery	-2.40	1.39	.429	-6.35	1.55
	Intentional	-1.00	1.39	.951	-4.95	2.95
Imagery	Counting	6.40*	1.39	.000	2.45	10.35
	Rhyming	6.50*	1.39	.000	2.55	10.45
	Adjective	2.40	1.39	.429	-1.55	6.35
	Intentional	1.40	1.39	.851	-2.55	5.35
Intentional	Counting	5.00*	1.39	.007	1.05	8.95
	Rhyming	5.10*	1.39	.006	1.15	9.05
	Adjective	1.00	1.39	.951	-2.95	4.95
	Imagery	-1.40	1.39	.851	-5.35	2.55

*. The mean difference is significant at the .05 level.

12.13 For Tukey's HSD test:

Table (1), (2), and (4) are the same as found in Exercise 12.12. In (3) the values are based on df' and $r = 5$.

66

(3) Matrix of q_{HSD}:

Group	1	2	3	4	5
1	--	4.89	4.41	4.45	4.37
2		--	4.76	4.89	4.76
3			--	4.45	4.37
4				--	4.41
5					--

The critical values are not constant because df' varies. All are taken at $r = 5$.

(5)   Matrix of W_r = product of corresponding elements of (3) & (4):

Group	1	2	3	4	5
1	--	5.67	4.41	4.41	4.33
2		--	5.66	5.77	5.66
3			--	4.58	4.50
4				--	4.50
5					--

The same pattern of significance is found as in Exercise 12.12.

12.15 Tukey's HSD test applied to the THC data in Table 11.5

Group:	1	2	3	4	5
µg THC	0	0.1	0.5	1	2
n_j	10	10	9	8	10

$$n_h = \frac{k}{\Sigma(\frac{1}{n_j})} = \frac{5}{\frac{1}{10} + \frac{1}{10} + \frac{1}{9} + \frac{1}{8} + \frac{1}{10}} = 9.326$$

Group	1	5	4	2	3	r	q_{HSD}	W_r
Means	34.00	38.10	18.50	50.80	60.33			
1	--	4.1	14.5	16.8	26.33*	5	4.04	20.51
5		--	10.4	12.7	22.23*	4	4.04	20.51
4			--	2.3	11.83	3	4.04	20.51
2				--	9.53	2	4.04	20.51
3					--			

$$w_r = q_{.05}(r, df)\sqrt{\frac{MS_{error}}{N_h}} = 4.04\sqrt{\frac{240.35}{9.326}} = 20.51$$

The 0.5µg group is different from the control group and the 2µg group. No other differences not significant. The maximum familywise error rate is .05.

12.17 If you are willing to sacrifice using a common error term, you simply run the relevant t tests but evaluate them at $\alpha' = \alpha/c$.

12.19 Linear and quadratic trend in Conti and Musty (1984).

The results given below assume that you have added the three observations mentioned in the exercise.

Group:	Control	0.1	0.5	1	2	
Means:	34.00	50.80	60.33	48.50	38.10	
Linear	-0.72	-0.62	-0.22	0.28	1.28	$\Sigma a_j^2 = 2.66$
Quadratic	0.389	0.199	-0.362	-0.612	0.387	$\Sigma b_j^2 = 0.84$

$$L_{Linear} = \Sigma a_j \overline{X}_j = -.72(34.00) - .62(50.80) - .22(60.33) + .28(48.50)$$
$$+ 1.28(38.10) = -6.901$$

$$L_{Quad} = \Sigma b_j \overline{X}_j = .389(34.00) + .199(50.80) - .362(60.33)$$
$$- .612(48.50) + .387(38.10) = -13.44$$

$$SS_{Linear} = \frac{nL^2}{\Sigma a_j^2} = \frac{10(-6.901^2)}{2.668} = 178.479$$

$$SS_{Quad} = \frac{nL^2}{\Sigma b_j^2} = \frac{10(-13.44^2)}{.846} = 2135.645$$

Source	*df*		SS	MS	*F*
Treatments	4		4396.12	1099.03	4.90*
Linear		1	178.48	178.48	<1
Quadratic		1	2135.64	2135.64	9.52*
Error	45		10095.10	224.34	
Total	49		14491.22		

There is a significant quadratic trend, but no significant linear trend. This quadratic trend is clearly visible in the means.

12.21 Computer example.

12.23 Trend analysis for Epineq.dat separately at each interval.

12.23 Trend analysis for Epineq.dat separately at each interval.

One Day: $F_{Linear} = 9.44$ (p = .0042); $F_{Quad} = 20.43$ (p = .0001)

One Week: $F_{Linear} = 4.33$ (p = .0453); $F_{Quad} = 13.23$ (p = .0009)

One Month: $F_{Linear} = 6.91$ (p = .0129); $F_{Quad} = 8.60$ (p = .0061)

12.25 Stone et al. (1992): Glucose and memory:

a.

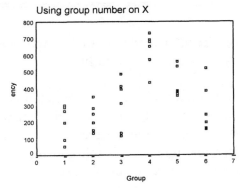 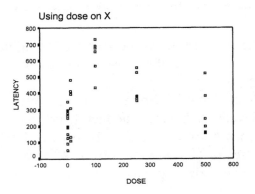

b. Trend analysis using actual dose:

ANOVA

LATENCY

			Sum of Squares	df	Mean Square	F	Sig.
Between Groups	(Combined)		772106.472	5	154421.294	11.193	.000
	Linear Term	Contrast	7561.039	1	7561.039	.548	.465
		Deviation	764545.433	4	191136.358	13.855	.000
Within Groups			413869.833	30	13795.661		
Total			1185976.306	35			

c. Trend analysis using 1, 2, ...6 as coding:

ANOVA

LATENCY

			Sum of Squares	df	Mean Square	F	Sig.
Between Groups	(Combined)		772106.472	5	154421.294	11.193	.000
	Linear Term	Contrast	152114.402	1	152114.402	11.026	.002
		Deviation	619992.070	4	154998.017	11.235	.000
Within Groups			413869.833	30	13795.661		
Total			1185976.306	35			

d. When we use the group number coding in our trend analysis we find a significant linear trend. As the dose of sucrose increases, memory increases accordingly.

e. The choice of coding system in not always obvious. Using 1, 2, ... ,6 actually ranks the dose levels and ignores the fact that dose increases in an extreme way. (In other words, the difference between the first 1 doses is 1 mg/kg, whereas the difference between the last two doses is 250 mg/kg. Using 1, 2, ..., 6 deliberately ignores this relationship. Apparently the human body responds in a nonlinear way to the increase in actual dose levels.

12.27 The Newman-Keuls error rate is greater than $\alpha = .05$ when the overall null is false because there are more than one possibly true null hypotheses among the set of means. Each true null has a probability of .05 of being rejected. Ryan's test corrects for the lack of control of the familywise error rate in this situation by using a more appropriate adjustment of the size of the critical region as r increases.

Chapter 13 - Factorial Analysis of Variance

Note: Because of severe rounding in reporting and using means, there will be visible rounding error in the following answers, when compared to standard computer solutions. I have made the final answer equal the correct answer, even if that meant that it is not exactly the answer to the calculations shown. (e.g. 3(3.3) would be shown as 10.0, not 9.9)

13.1 Mother/infant interaction for primiparous/multiparous mothers under or over 18 years of age with LBW or full-term infants:

Table of cell means

		Size/Age			
		LBW < 18	LBW > 18	NBW	
Mother's	Primi-	4.5	5.3	6.4	5.40
Parity	Multi-	3.9	6.9	8.2	6.33
		4.2	6.1	7.3	5.87

$$SS_{total} = \Sigma X^2 - \frac{(\Sigma X)^2}{N} = 2404 - \frac{352^2}{60} = 338.93$$

$$SS_{Parity} = ns\Sigma\left(\overline{X}_{i.} - \overline{X}_{..}\right)^2$$

$$= 10(3)[(5.40 - 5.87)^2 + (6.33 - 5.87)^2]$$

$$= 30(0.4356) = 13.067$$

$$SS_{size} = np\Sigma\left(\overline{X}_{.j} - \overline{X}_{..}\right)^2$$

$$= 10(2)[(4.200 - 5.87)^2 + (6.10 - 5.87)^2 + (7.30 - 5.87)^2]$$

$$= 20(2.79 + 0.05 + 2.04) = 20(4.89)$$

$$= 97.733$$

$$SS_{cells} = n\Sigma\left(\overline{X}_{ij} - \overline{X}_{..}\right)^2$$

$$= 10[(4.5 - 5.87)^2 + ... + (8.2 - 5.87)^2]$$

$$= 10(12.853) = 128.53$$

$$SS_{PS} = SS_{cells} - SS_P - SS_S = 128.53 - 13.067 - 97.733$$

$$= 17.733$$

$$SS_{error} = SS_{total} - SS_{cells} = 338.93 - 128.53$$

$$= 210.40$$

Source	df	SS	MS	F
Parity	1	13.067	13.067	3.354
Size/Age	2	97.733	48.867	12.541*
P x S	2	17.733	8.867	2.276
Error	54	210.400	3.896	
Total	59	338.933		

*$p < .05$ $F_{.05}(2,54) = 3.17$

13.3 The mean for these primiparous mothers would not be expected to be a good estimate of the mean for the population of all primiparous mothers because 50% of the population of primiparous mothers do not give birth to LBW infants. This would be important if we wished to take means from this sample as somehow representing the population means for primiparous and multiparous mothers.

13.5 Memory of avoidance of a fear-producing stimulus:

		Neutral	Area A	Area B	Mean
	50	28.6	16.8	24.4	23.27
Delay	100	28.0	23.0	16.0	22.33
	150	28.0	26.8	26.4	27.07
	Mean	28.2	22.2	22.27	24.22

Area of Stimulation

$\Sigma X = 1090$ $\Sigma X^2 = 28374$ $N = 45$ $n = 5$ $a = 3$ $d = 3$

$$SS_{total} = \Sigma X^2 - \frac{(\Sigma X)^2}{N} = 28374 - \frac{1090^2}{45} = 1971.778$$

$$SS_{Delay} = na\Sigma\left(\bar{X}_{i.} - \bar{X}_{..}\right)^2$$

$$= 5(3)[(23.27 - 24.22)^2 + (22.33 - 24.22)^2 + (27.07 - 24.22)^2]$$

$$= 5(3)(0.90 + 3.57 + 8.12) = 30(12.60)$$

$$= 188.578$$

$$SS_{Area} = nd\Sigma\left(\bar{X}_{.j} - \bar{X}_{..}\right)^2$$

$$= 5(3)[(28.20 - 24.22)^2 + (22.20 - 24.22)^2 + (22.27 - 24.22)^2]$$

$$= 356.044$$

$$SS_{Cells} = n\Sigma\left(\bar{X}_{ij} - \bar{X}_{..}\right)^2$$

$$= 5[(28.60 - 24.22)^2 + (16.80 - 24.22)^2 + ... + (26.4 - 24.22)^2]$$

$$= 916.578$$

$$SS_{DA} = SS_{cells} - SS_D - SS_A = 916.578 - 188.578 - 356.044 = 371.956$$

$$SS_{error} = SS_{total} - SS_{cells} = 1971.778 - 916.578 = 1055.200$$

Source	df	SS	MS	F
Delay	2	188.578	94.289	3.22
Area	2	356.044	178.022	6.07*
D x A	4	371.956	92.989	3.17*
Error	36	1055.200	29.311	
Total	44	1971.778		

$*p < .05 \quad [F_{.05(2,36)} = 3.27; \ F_{.05(4,36)} = 2.64]$

13.7 In Exercise 13.5, if A refers to Area:

$\hat{\alpha}_1$ = the treatment effect for the Neutral site

$$= \bar{X}_{.1} - \bar{X}_{..}$$

$$= 28.2 - 24.22 = 3.978$$

13.9 The Bonferroni test to compare Site means.

$$t = \frac{\overline{N} - \overline{A}}{\sqrt{\dfrac{MS_{error}}{n_N} + \dfrac{MS_{error}}{n_A}}} \qquad t = \frac{\overline{N} - \overline{B}}{\sqrt{\dfrac{MS_{error}}{n_N} + \dfrac{MS_{error}}{n_B}}}$$

$$= \frac{28.20 - 22.20}{\sqrt{\dfrac{29.311}{15} + \dfrac{29.311}{15}}} \qquad = \frac{28.20 - 22.27}{\sqrt{\dfrac{29.311}{15} + \dfrac{29.311}{15}}}$$

$$= 3.03 \ (\text{Reject } H_0) \qquad = 3.00 \ (\text{Reject } H_0)$$

$[t'_{.025}(2,36) = \pm 2.34]$

We can conclude that both the difference between Groups N and A and between Groups N and B are significant, and our familywise error rate will not exceed $\alpha = .05$.

13.11 Rerunning Exercise 11.3 as a factorial design:

The following printout is from SPSS

Tests of Between-Subjects Effects

Dependent Variable: RECALL

Source	Type III Sum of Squares	df	Mean Square	F	Sig.
Corrected Model	1945.490[a]	9	216.166	26.935	.000
Intercept	13479.210	1	13479.210	1679.536	.000
AGE	240.250	1	240.250	29.936	.000
CONDTION	1514.940	4	378.735	47.191	.000
AGE * CONDTION	190.300	4	47.575	5.928	.000
Error	722.300	90	8.026		
Total	16147.000	100			
Corrected Total	2667.790	99			

a. R Squared = .729 (Adjusted R Squared = .702)

[The Corrected Model is the sum of the main effects and interaction. The Intercept is the correction factor, which is $(\Sigma X)^2$. The Total (as opposed to Corrected Total) is ΣX^2. The Corrected Total is what we have called Total.]

Estimated Marginal Means

AGE * CONDTION

Dependent Variable: RECALL

AGE	CONDTION	Mean	Std. Error	95% Confidence Interval	
				Lower Bound	Upper Bound
Older	Counting	7.000	.896	5.220	8.780
	Rhyming	6.900	.896	5.120	8.680
	Adjective	11.000	.896	9.220	12.780
	Imagery	13.400	.896	11.620	15.180
	Intentional	12.000	.896	10.220	13.780
Young	Counting	6.500	.896	4.720	8.280
	Rhyming	7.600	.896	5.820	9.380
	Adjective	14.800	.896	13.020	16.580
	Imagery	17.600	.896	15.820	19.380
	Intentional	19.300	.896	17.520	21.080

["Condition" is spelled as "Condtion" because the maximum length is 8 characters.]

The results show that there is a significance difference between younger and older subjects, that there is better recall in tasks which require more processing, and that there

74

is an interaction between age and level of processing (Condition). The difference between the two levels of processing is greater for the younger subjects than it is for the older ones, primarily because the older ones do not do much better with greater amounts of processing.

13.13 Made-up data with main effects but no interaction:

Cell means: 8   12
              4   6

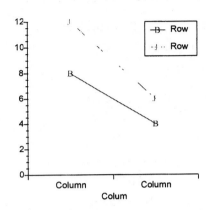

13.15 The interaction was of primary interest in an experiment by Nisbett in which he showed that obese people varied the amount of food they consumed depending on whether a lot or a little food was visible, while normal weight subjects ate approximately the same amount under the two conditions.

13.17 Unequal sample sizes in hospital patients responses to two different therapies:

Cell *ns*:

		Treatment		
		A	B	
Hospital	#1	3	6	9
	#2	2	4	6
		5	10	15 = $\sum X$

$$\overline{N}_h = \frac{k}{\sum \frac{1}{n_i}} = \frac{4}{\frac{1}{3} + \frac{1}{6} + \frac{1}{2} + \frac{1}{4}} = 3.2$$

Cell Means:

		Treatment		
		A	B	
Hospital	#1	6.33	11.00	8.665
	#2	11.00	27.25	19.125
		8.665	19.125	13.895

$$SS_H = tn_h\Sigma\left(\bar{X}_{i.} - \bar{X}_{..}\right)^2 = 2*3.2\left[\left(8.665 - 13.895\right)^2 + \left(19.125 - 13.895\right)^2\right]$$
$$= 350.117$$

$$SS_T = hn_h\Sigma\left(\bar{X}_{.j} - \bar{X}_{..}\right)^2 = 2*3.2\left[\left(8.665 - 13.895\right)^2 + \left(19.125 - 13.895\right)^2\right]$$
$$= 350.117$$

$$SS_{cells} = n_h\Sigma\left(\bar{X}_{ij} - \bar{X}_{..}\right)^2 = 3.2\left[\left(6.33 - 13.895\right)^2 + ... + \left(27.25 - 13.895\right)^2\right]$$
$$= 807.429$$

$$SS_{HT} = SS_{cells} - SS_H - SS_T = 807.429 - 350.117 - 350.117 = 107.195$$

Cell variances:

		Treatment	
		A	B
Hospital	#1	2.333	4.400
	#2	2.000	72.917

$$SS_{error} = \Sigma(n_{ij} - 1)s_{ij}^2 = 2(2.333) + 5(4.400) + 1(2.000) + 3(72.917) = 247.417$$

Source	df	SS	MS	F
Hospital	1	350.117	350.117	15.57*
Therapy	1	350.117	350.117	15.57*
H X T	1	107.195	107.195	4.77
Error	11	247.417	22.492	
Total	14			

$*p < .05$ $[F_{.05(1,11)} = 4.84]$

We can conclude that there are effects due to both Hospital and Therapy, but there is no interaction between the two main effect variables. (Notice the heterogeneity of variance.)

It is instructive to compare this result (which produces equal effects for rows and columns) with the result that we would achieve if we just took the average of the observations in the rows (or columns). If we did that we would see that the difference between the row means (9.44 and 21.83) is more than the difference we would find between the column means (8.2 and 17.5).

13.19   Magnitude of effect for mother-infant interaction data in Exercise 13.1:

$$\eta_P^2 = \frac{SS_{parity}}{SS_{total}} = \frac{13.067}{338.933} = .04$$

$$\eta_S^2 = \frac{SS_{size}}{SS_{total}} = \frac{97.733}{338.933} = .29$$

$$\eta_{PS}^2 = \frac{SS_{PS}}{SS_{total}} = \frac{17.733}{338.933} = .05$$

$$\omega_P^2 = \frac{SS_{parity} - (p-1)MS_{error}}{SS_{total} + MS_{error}} = \frac{13.067 - (1)(3.896)}{338.933 + 3.896} = .03$$

$$\omega_S^2 = \frac{SS_{size} - (s-1)MS_{error}}{SS_{total} + MS_{error}} = \frac{97.733 - (2)(3.896)}{338.933 + 3.896} = .26$$

$$\omega_{PS}^2 = \frac{SS_{PS} - (p-1)(s-1)MS_{error}}{SS_{total} + MS_{error}} = \frac{17.733 - (1)(2)(3.896)}{338.933 + 3.896} = .03$$

13.21   Three-way ANOVA on Early Experience x Intensity of UCS x Conditioned Stimulus (Tone or Vibration):

$n = 5$ in all cells $SS_{total} = 41,151.00$

E×I×C Cells

Exper:	CS = Tone Hi	Med	Low			CS = Vibration Hi	Med	Low		
Control	11	16	21	12.0		19	24	29	24.00	20.00
Tone	25	28	34	29.0		21	26	31	26.00	27.50
Vib	6	13	20	13.0		40	41	52	44.33	28.67
Both	22	30	30	27.33		35	38	48	40.33	33.83
	16	21.75	105	21.33		28.75	32.25	40.00	33.66	27.50

E×I Cells

Experience:	Intensity High	Med	Low	
Control	15	20	25	20.00
Tone	23	27	32.5	27.50
Vib	23	27	36	28.67
Both	28.5	34	39	33.83
	22.38	27.00	33.12	27.50

E×C Cells

	Conditioned Stimulus		
Experience:	Tone	Vib	
Control	16.00	24.00	20.00
Tone	29.00	26.00	27.50
Vib	13.00	44.33	28.67
Both	27.33	40.33	33.83
	21.33	33.66	27.50

I×C Cells

	Conditioned Stim		
Intensity:	Tone	Vib	
High	16.00	28.75	22.38
Med	21.75	32.25	27.00
Low	26.25	40.00	33.12
	21.33	33.67	27.50

$$SS_E = nic\Sigma\left(\bar{X}_{i..} - \bar{X}_{...}\right)^2 = 5(3)(2)\left[\begin{array}{l}(20-27.5)^2 + (27.5-27.5)^2 + (28.67-27.5)^2 + \\ (33.83-27.5)^2\end{array}\right]$$

$$= 2931.667$$

$$SS_I = nec\Sigma\left(\bar{X}_{.j.} - \bar{X}_{...}\right)^2 = 5(4)(2)\left[\begin{array}{l}(22.38-27.5)^2 + (27.00-27.5)^2 + \\ (33.12-27.5)^2\end{array}\right]$$

$$= 2326.250$$

$$SS_{cellsEI} = nc\Sigma\left(\bar{X}_{ij.} - \bar{X}_{...}\right)^2 = (5)(2)\left[(15.00-27.50)^2 + ... + (39.00-27.50)^2\right]$$

$$= 5325.000$$

$$SS_{E\times I} = SS_{cellsEI} - SS_E - SS_I = 5325.000 - 2931.667 - 2326.250 = 67.083$$

$$SS_C = nei\Sigma\left(\bar{X}_{..k} - \bar{X}_{...}\right)^2 = 5(4)(3)\left[(21.33-27.5)^2 + (33.66-27.5)^2\right]$$
$$= 4563.333$$

$$SS_{cellsEC} = ni\Sigma\left(\bar{X}_{i.k} - \bar{X}_{...}\right)^2 = (5)(3)\left[(16.00-27.50)^2 + ... + (40.33-27.50)^2\right]$$
$$= 12,110.000$$

$$SS_{E\times C} = SS_{cellsEC} - SS_E - SS_C = 12,110.000 - 2931.667 - 4563.333 = 4615.000$$

$$SS_{cellsIC} = ne\Sigma\left(\bar{X}_{ij.} - \bar{X}_{...}\right)^2 = (5)(4)\left[(15.00-27.50)^2 + ... + (39.00-27.50)^2\right]$$
$$= 6945.000$$

$$SS_{I\times C} = SS_{cellsIC} - SS_I - SS_C = 6945.000 - 2326.250 - 4563.333 = 55.417$$

$$SS_{cellsEIC} = n\Sigma\left(\bar{X}_{ijk} - \bar{X}_{...}\right)^2 = (5)\left[(11.00-27.50)^2 + ... + (48.00-27.50)^2\right]$$
$$= 14,680.000$$

$$SS_{E\times I\times C} = SS_{cellsEIC} - SS_E - SS_I - SS_C - SS_{EI} - SS_{EC} - SS_{IC}$$
$$= 14,680.000 - 2931.667 - 2326.250 - 4563.333 - 67.083 - 4615.000 - 55.417$$
$$= 121.25$$

$$SS_{error} = SS_{total} - SS_{CellsC\times E\times I} = 41,151.000 - 14,680.000 = 26.471.000$$

Source	df	SS	MS	F
Experience	3	2931.667	977.222	3.544*
Intensity	2	2326.250	1163.125	4.218*
Cond Stim	1	4563.333	4563.333	16.550*
E x I	6	67.083	11.181	<1
E x C	3	4615.000	1538.333	5.579*
I x C	2	55.417	27.708	<1
E x I x C	6	121.250	20.208	<1
Error	96	26,471.000	275.740	
Total	119	41,151.000		

$*p<.05$ $[F_{.05\,(1,96)} = 3.94;\ F_{.05\,(2,96)} = 3.09;\ F_{.05\,(3,96)} = 2.70;\ F_{.05\,(6,96)} = 2.19]$

There are significant main effects for all variables with a significant Experience × Conditioned Stimulus interaction.

13.23   Analysis of Epineq.dat:

Tests of Between-Subjects Effects

Dependent Variable: Trials to reversal

Source	Type III Sum of Squares	df	Mean Square	F	Sig.
Corrected Model	141.130[a]	8	17.641	8.158	.000
Intercept	1153.787	1	1153.787	533.554	.000
DOSE	133.130	2	66.565	30.782	.000
DELAY	2.296	2	1.148	.531	.590
DOSE * DELAY	5.704	4	1.426	.659	.622
Error	214.083	99	2.162		
Total	1509.000	108			
Corrected Total	355.213	107			

a. R Squared = .397 (Adjusted R Squared = .349)

13.25   Tukey on Dosage data from Exercise 13.23

Multiple Comparisons

Dependent Variable: Trials to reversal
Tukey HSD

(I) dosage of epinephrine	(J) dosage of epinephrine	Mean Difference (I-J)	Std. Error	Sig.
0.0 mg/kg	0.3 mg/kg	-1.67*	.35	.000
	1.0 mg/kg	1.03*	.35	.010
0.3 mg/kg	0.0 mg/kg	1.67*	.35	.000
	1.0 mg/kg	2.69*	.35	.000
1.0 mg/kg	0.0 mg/kg	-1.03*	.35	.010
	0.3 mg/kg	-2.69*	.35	.000

Based on observed means.

*. The mean difference is significant at the .05 level.

All of these groups differed from each other at $p \leq .05$.

13.27 Simple effects on data in Exercise 13.26.

Source	df	SS	MS	F
Condition	1	918.750	918.75	34.42*
Cond @ Inexp.	1	1014.00	1014.00	37.99*
Cond @ Exp.	1	121.50	121.50	4.55*
Cond*Exper	1	216.750	216.75	8.12*
Other Effects	9	2631.417		
Error	36	961.000	26.694	
Total	47	4727.917		

$*p < .05; F_{.05(1,36)} = 4.12$

Chapter 14 – Repeated-Measures Designs

[As in previous chapters, there will be substantial rounding in these answers. I have attempted to make the answers fit with the correct values, rather than the exact results of the specific calculations shown here. Thus I may round cell means to two decimals, but calculation is carried out with many more decimals.]

14.1 Does taking the GRE repeatedly lead to higher scores?

a. Statistical model:

$$X_{ij} = \mu + \pi_i + \tau_j + \pi\tau_{ij} + e_{ij} \text{ or } X_{ij} = \mu + \pi_i + \tau_j + e_{ij}'$$

b. Analysis:

Subject	Mean		Test Session	Mean
1	566.67		1	552.50
2	450.00		2	563.75
3	616.67		3	573.75
4	663.33			
5	436.67			
6	696.67			
7	503.33			
8	573.33			
Mean	563.33			

$$SS_{total} = \Sigma X^2 - \frac{(\Sigma X)^2}{N}$$

$$= 7811200 - \frac{(13520)^2}{24} = 194933.33$$

$$SS_{subj} = t\Sigma(\bar{X}_{i.} - \bar{X}_{..})^2$$

$$= 3[(566.67 - 563.33)^2 + ... + (573.33 - 563.33)^2] = 3(63,222.22) = 189,666.67$$

$$SS_{test} = n\Sigma(\bar{X}_{.j} - \bar{X}_{..})^2 = 8[(552.50 - 563.33)^2 + (563.75 - 563.33)^2 + (573.75 - 563.33)^2]$$

$$= 8[226.04] = 1808.33$$

$$SS_{error} = SS_{total} - SS_{subj} - SS_{test}$$

$$= 194,933.33 - 189,666.67 - 1808.33 = 3458.33$$

Source	df	SS	MS	F
Subjects	7	189,666.66		
Within Subj	16	5266.67		
Test Session	2	1808.33	904.17	3.66 ns
Error	14	3458.33	247.02	
Total	23	194,933.33		

14.3 Teaching of self-care skills to severely retarded children:

Cell means:

		Baseline	Training	Mean
		Phase		
Group:	Exp	4.80	7.00	5.90
	Control	4.70	6.40	5.55
	Mean	4.75	6.70	5.72

Subject means:

		S_1	S_2	S_3	S_4	S_5	S_6	S_7	S_8	S_9	S_{10}
Grp	Exp	8.5	6.0	2.5	6.0	5.5	6.5	6.5	5.5	5.5	6.5
	Control	4.0	5.0	9.0	3.5	4.0	8.0	7.5	4.5	5.0	5.5

$\Sigma X^2 = 1501$ $\Sigma X = 229$ $N = 40$ $n = 10$ $g = 2$ $p = 2$

$$SS_{total} = \Sigma X^2 - \frac{(\Sigma X)^2}{N} = 1501 - \frac{(229)^2}{40} = 189.975$$

$$SS_{subj} = p\Sigma\left(\bar{X}_{ij.} - \bar{X}_{...}\right)^2$$
$$= 2[(8.5-5.72)^2 + ... + (5.5-5.72)^2] = 106.475$$

$$SS_{group} = pn\Sigma\left(\bar{X}_{..k} - \bar{X}_{...}\right)^2$$
$$= 2(8)[(5.90-5.72)^2 + (5.55-5.72)^2] = 1.225$$

$$SS_{phase} = gn\Sigma\left(\bar{X}_{.j.} - \bar{X}_{...}\right)^2$$
$$= 2(10)[(4.75-5.72)^2 + (6.70-5.72)^2] = 38.025$$

$$SS_{cells} = n\Sigma\left(\bar{X}_{.jk} - \bar{X}_{...}\right)^2$$
$$= 10\left[(4.80-5.72)^2 + ... + (6.40-5.72)^2\right] = 39.875$$

$$SS_{PG} = SS_{cells} - SS_{phase} - SS_{group} = 39.875 - 38.025 - 1.225 = 0.925$$

Source	df	SS	MS	F
Between Subj	19	106.475		
Groups	1	1.125	1.125	0.19
Ss w/in Grps	18	105.250	5.847	
Within Subj	20	83.500		
Phase	1	38.025	38.025	15.26*
P x G	1	0.625	0.625	0.25
P x Ss w/in Grps	18	44.850	2.492	
Total	39	189.975		

$*p < .05$ $[F_{.05(1,18)} = 4.41]$

There is a significant difference between baseline and training, but there are no group differences nor a group x phase interaction.

14.5 Adding a No Attention control group to the study in Exercise 14.3:

Cell means:

		Phase		
		Baseline	Training	Total
Group	Exp	4.8	7.0	5.90
	Att Cont	4.7	6.4	5.55
	No Att Cont	5.1	4.6	4.85
	Total	4.87	6.00	5.43

Subject means:

Group:		S_1	S_2	S_3	S_4	S_5	S_6	S_7	S_8	S_9	S_{10}
	Exp	8.5	6.0	2.5	6.0	5.5	6.5	6.5	5.5	5.5	6.5
	Att Cont	4.0	5.0	9.0	3.5	4.0	8.0	7.5	4.5	5.0	5.0
	No Att Cont	3.5	5.0	7.0	5.5	4.5	6.5	6.5	4.5	2.5	3.0

$$\Sigma X^2 = 2026 \qquad \Sigma X = 326 \qquad N = 60 \qquad n = 10 \qquad g = 3 \qquad p = 2$$

$$SS_{Total} = \Sigma X^2 - \frac{(\Sigma X)^2}{N} = 2026 - \frac{(326)^2}{40} = 254.7333$$

$$SS_{subj} = p\Sigma\left(\bar{X}_{ij.} - \bar{X}_{...}\right)^2$$
$$= 2[(8.5 - 5.43)^2 + ... + (3.0 - 5.43)^2] = 159.733$$

$$SS_{groups} = pn\Sigma\left(\bar{X}_{..k} - \bar{X}_{...}\right)^2$$
$$= 2(8)[(5.90 - 5.43)^2 + (5.55 - 5.43)^2 + (4.85 - 5.43)^2] = 11.433$$

$$SS_{phase} = gn\Sigma\left(\bar{X}_{.j.} - \bar{X}_{...}\right)^2$$
$$= 3(10)[(4.87 - 5.43)^2 + (6.00 - 5.43)^2] = 19.267$$

$$SS_{cells} = n\Sigma\left(\bar{X}_{.jk} - \bar{X}_{...}\right)^2$$
$$= 10\left[(4.80 - 5.43)^2 + ... + (4.60 - 5.43)^2\right] = 52.333$$

$$SS_{PG} = SS_{cells} - SS_{phase} - SS_{group} = 51.333 - 19.267 - 11.433 = 20.633$$

Source	df	SS	MS	F
Between Subj	29	159.7333		
Groups	2	11.4333	5.7166	1.04
Ss w/ Grps	27	148.300	5.4926	
Within Subj	30	95.0000		
Phase	1	19.2667	19.2667	9.44*
P * G	2	20.6333	10.3165	5.06*
P * Ss w/Grps	27	55.1000	2.0407	
Total	59	254.733		

$*p < .05 \quad [F_{.05\,(1,27)} = 4.22; F_{.05\,(2,27)} = 3.36]$

b. Plot:

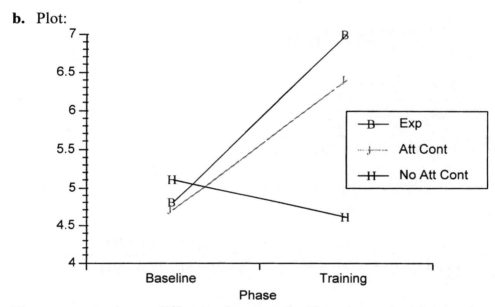

c. There seems to be no difference between the Experimental and Attention groups, but both show significantly more improvement than the No Attention group.

14.7 For the data in Exercise 14.6:

a. Variance-covariance matrices:

$$\hat{\Sigma}_{owners} = \begin{bmatrix} 1.30 & 1.50 & 0.75 \\ 1.50 & 2.00 & 1.00 \\ 0.75 & 1.00 & 1.00 \end{bmatrix}$$

$$\hat{\Sigma}_{non\text{-}owners} = \begin{bmatrix} 2.70 & 1.20 & 1.85 \\ 1.20 & 0.70 & 0.60 \\ 1.85 & 0.60 & 3.30 \end{bmatrix}$$

$$\hat{\Sigma}_{pooled} = \begin{bmatrix} 2.00 & 1.35 & 1.30 \\ 1.35 & 1.35 & 0.80 \\ 1.30 & 0.80 & 2.15 \end{bmatrix} \begin{matrix} \overline{s}_j \\ 1.550 \\ 1.167 \\ 1.417 \end{matrix}$$

$$\hat{\Sigma}_{between} = \begin{bmatrix} 4.50 & 9.00 & 34.50 \\ 9.00 & 18.00 & 69.00 \\ 34.50 & 69.00 & 264.50 \end{bmatrix}$$

b. $\hat{e}$

$$\overline{s}_{jj} = \frac{2.00 + 1.35 + 2.15}{3} = 1.833$$

$$\overline{s} = \frac{2.00 + \ldots + 2.15}{9} = 1.378$$

$$\Sigma s_{jk}^2 = 2.00^2 + \ldots + 2.15^2 = 18.750$$

$$\Sigma \overline{s}_j^2 = 1.550^2 + 1.167^2 1.417^2 = 18.750$$

$$\hat{e} = \frac{b^2 \left(\overline{s}_{jj} - \overline{s} \right)^2}{(b-1)\left(\Sigma s_{jk}^2 - 2b\Sigma \overline{s}_j^2 + b^2 \overline{s}^2 \right)} = \frac{9(1.833 - 1.378)^2}{2\left[18.75 - 6(5.772) + 9\left(1.378^2 \right) \right]}$$

14.9 Back to the calculator usage data in Exercise 14.6:

a. Plot

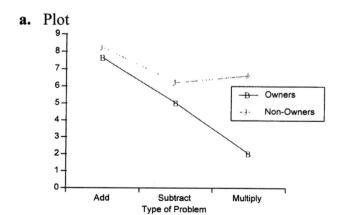

b. Analysis of simple effects:

Cell means:	Problems			
	Add	Subt	Mult	Mean
Owners	7.6	5.0	2.0	4.87
Non-Owners	8.2	6.2	6.6	7.00
Mean	7.9	5.6	4.3	5.935

For the first three simple effects we're breaking down a combination of SS_{Groups} and SS_{PG} from the overall analysis in Exercise 14.6, so for the error term we will need to combine the error terms which were used to test MS_{Groups} and MS_{PG} in that analysis.

$$MS_{w/in\,Cell} = \frac{MS_{Ss\,w/in\,grps} + MS_{P*Ss\,w/in\,grps}}{df_{Ss\,w/in\,grps} + df_{P*Ss\,w/in\,grps}} = \frac{33.066 + 10.934}{8 + 16} = 1.833$$

The df against which to evaluate F also must be adjusted for these simple effects. F_{obt} will be evaluated against $F_{.05(g-1,\,f')}$ but we must first calculate f '.

$$f' = \frac{(u+v)^2}{\frac{u^2}{df_u} + \frac{v^2}{df_v}} = \frac{(33.066 + 10.934)^2}{\frac{33.066^2}{8} + \frac{10.934^2}{16}} = 13.431 \quad u = SS_{Ss\,w/in\,grps}$$

$$v = SS_{P*Ss\,w/in\,grps}$$

With the error terms and degrees of freedom ready, we go ahead with calculating the sums of squares and testing them:

$$SS_{group\,at\,Add} = n\Sigma\left(\bar{X}_{i1} - \bar{X}_{.1}\right)^2$$
$$= 5[(7.6 - 7.9)^2 + (8.2 - 7.9)^2] = 0.9$$

$$MS_{group\,at\,Add} = \frac{SS_{group\,at\,Add}}{df_{group\,at\,Add}} = \frac{0.9}{1} = 0.9$$

$$F_{group\,at\,Add} = \frac{MS_{group\,at\,Add}}{MS_{w/in\,cells}} = \frac{0.9}{1.833} = <1$$

$$SS_{group\,at\,Subt} = n\Sigma\left(\bar{X}_{i2} - \bar{X}_{.2}\right)^2$$
$$= 5[(5.0 - 5.6)^2 + (6.0 - 5.6)^2] = 3.6$$

$$MS_{group\,at\,Subt} = \frac{SS_{group\,at\,Subt}}{df_{group\,at\,Subt}} = \frac{3.6}{1} = 3.6$$

$$F_{group\,at\,Subt} = \frac{MS_{group\,at\,Subt}}{MS_{w/in\,cells}} = \frac{3.6}{1.833} = 1.96ns$$

$$SS_{group\ at\ Mult} = n\Sigma\left(\bar{X}_{i3} - \bar{X}_{.3}\right)^2$$

$$= 5[(2.0 - 4.3)^2 + (6.6 - 4.3)^2] = 52.9$$

$$MS_{group\ at\ Mult} = \frac{SS_{group\ at\ Mult}}{df_{group\ at\ Mult}} = \frac{52.9}{1} = 52.9$$

$$F_{group\ at\ Mult} = \frac{MS_{group\ at\ Mult}}{MS_{w/in\ cells}} = \frac{52.9}{1.833} = 28.86*$$

$$*p < .05 \quad [F_{.05\,(g-1,\,r)} = F_{.05\,(1,\,13)} = 4.67]$$

For the last two simple effects we're breaking down a combination of $SS_{Problems}$ and SS_{PG} from the overall analysis in Exercise 14.6. Since $MS_{Problems}$ and MS_{PG} were both tested by the same error term in that analysis ($MS_{P*Ss\ w/in\ grps}$) we could use that error term to test these simple effects. However, as pointed out in the chapter, violations of sphericity create serious problems when testing simple effects, and for that reason we will use separate error terms for the two analyses. The easiest way to do this is to run separate repeated measures analysis of variance for each group. This will produce the same sums of squares for the simple effect, as well as the appropriate error term.

The following results were produced by SPSS. Notice that the form of the printout is quite different from what we usually have. The corrected df (assuming a lack of sphericity) are given, as is the resulting significance level. (SPSS adjusts the two mean squares as the df are adjusted, but that does not alter the resulting F.)

Calculator owners:

Tests of Within-Subjects Effects[a]

Measure: MEASURE_1

Source		Type III Sum of Squares	df	Mean Square	F	Sig.
PROBLEM	Sphericity Assumed	78.533	2	39.267	112.190	.000
	Greenhouse-Geisser	78.533	1.477	53.157	112.190	.000
	Huynh-Feldt	78.533	2.000	39.267	112.190	.000
	Lower-bound	78.533	1.000	78.533	112.190	.000
Error(PROBLEM)	Sphericity Assumed	2.800	8	.350		
	Greenhouse-Geisser	2.800	5.910	.474		
	Huynh-Feldt	2.800	8.000	.350		
	Lower-bound	2.800	4.000	.700		

a. Calculator Owner = Owner

88

Non-owners

Measure: MEASURE_1

Source		Type III Sum of Squares	df	Mean Square	F	Sig.
PROBLEM	Sphericity Assumed	11.200	2	5.600	5.508	.031
	Greenhouse-Geisser	11.200	1.564	7.159	5.508	.047
	Huynh-Feldt	11.200	2.000	5.600	5.508	.031
	Lower-bound	11.200	1.000	11.200	5.508	.079
Error(PROBLEM)	Sphericity Assumed	8.133	8	1.017		
	Greenhouse-Geisser	8.133	6.258	1.300		
	Huynh-Feldt	8.133	8.000	1.017		
	Lower-bound	8.133	4.000	2.033		

a. Calculator Owner = NonOwner

The F is significant in both cases, indicating that Task made a difference. If we had used a pooled error term, MS_{error} would have been 0.683, which, because of the fact that the sample sizes were equal, is the average of the two error terms we used. But notice that the pooled error term would have been about 60% of what it was when we treat the groups separately.

14.11   From Exercise 14.10:
a.   Simple effect of reading ability for children:

$$SS_{RatC} = in\Sigma \left(\bar{X}_{RatC} - \bar{X}_C \right)^2$$
$$= 3(5)[(4.80 - 3.50)^2 + (2.20 - 3.50)^2] = 50.70$$
$$MS_{RatC} = \frac{SS_{RatC}}{df_{RatC}} = \frac{50.70}{1} = 50.70$$

Because we are using only the data from Children, it would be wise not to use a pooled error term. The following is the relevant printout from SPSS for the Between-subject effect of Reader.

Tests of Between-Subjects Effects[a]

Measure: MEASURE_1

Transformed Variable: Average

Source	Type III Sum of Squares	df	Mean Square	F	Sig.
Intercept	367.500	1	367.500	84.483	.000
READERS	50.700	1	50.700	11.655	.009
Error	34.800	8	4.350		

a. AGE = Children

b. Simple effect of items for adult good readers:

$$SS_{I \, at \, AG} = n\Sigma \left(\bar{X}_{I \, at \, AG} - \bar{X}_{AG} \right)^2$$
$$= 5[(6.20 - 5.73)^2 + (6.00 - 5.73)^2 + (5.00 - 5.73)^2] = 4.133$$

Again, we do not want to pool error terms. The following is the relevant printout from SPSS for Adult Good readers. The difference is not significant, nor would it be for any decrease in the *df* if we used a correction factor.

Tests of Within-Subjects Effects

Measure: MEASURE_1

Sphericity Assumed

Source	Type III Sum of Squares	df	Mean Square	F	Sig.
ITEMS	4.133	2	2.067	3.647	.075
Error(ITEMS)	4.533	8	.567		

14.13 It would certainly affect the covariances because we would force a high level of covariance among items. As the number of responses classified at one level of Item went up, another item would have to go down.

14.15 Plot of results in Exercise 14.14:

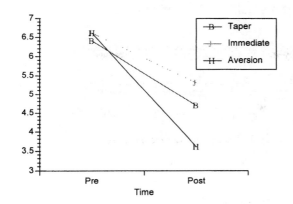

14.17 Analysis of data in Exercise 14.5 by BMDP:

    a. Comparison with results obtained by hand in Exercise 14.5.

    b. The F for Mean is a test on $H_0 : \mu = 0$.

    c. $MS_{w/in\ \text{Cell}}$ is the average of the cell variances.

14.19 Source column of summary table for 4-way ANOVA with repeated measures on A & B and independent measures on C & D.

Source
Between Ss
C
D
CD
Ss w/in groups
Within Ss
A
AC
AD
ACD
A x Ss w/in groups
B
BC
BD
BCD
B x Ss w/in groups
AB
ABC
ABD
$ABCD$
AB x Ss w/in groups
Total

14.21 Using Manova in Exercise 14.20 we have gained freedom from the sphericity assumption, but at the potential loss of a small amount of power.

14.23 Analysis of Stress data:

Source	df	SS	MS	F	Pillai F	Prob
Between Subj	97	137.683				
Gender	1	7.296	7.296	5.64*		
Role	1	8.402	8.402	6.49*		
G * R	1	0.298	0.298	<1		
Ss w/in Grps	94	121.687	1.294			
Within Subj	97	87.390				
Time	1	1.064	1.064	1.23*	1.23	0.2700
T*G	1	0.451	0.451	<1	0.52	0.4720
T*R	1	0.001	0.001	<1	0.00	0.9708
T*G*R	1	4.652	4.652	5.38*	5.38	0.0225
T*Ss w/in grps	94	81.222	0.864			
Total	194	103.386				

*$p < .05$

The univariate and multivariate F values agree because we have only two levels of each independent variable.

14.25 When multiple respondents come from the same family, their data are not likely to be independent. We act as if we have 98 different respondents, but in fact we do not have 98 *independent* respondents, which is important. If we had complete data from each family we could treat Spouse and Patient as a repeated measures variable—it is a "within-family" variable. Alternatively, we could delete data so as to have only one respondent per family. In this situation, numerous studies have shown that there is a remarkably small degree of dependence between members of the same family, and many people would ignore the problem entirely.

(The following questions appear to be ambiguous. 14.27 looks as if it is supposed to be part of 14.26, but the final manuscript is at the printer, and I can't check exactly.)

14.27 $t = -0.555$. There is no difference in Time 1 scores between those who did, and did not, have a score at Time 2.

14.29 (My copy shows a statement without a question, and 14.30 and those that follow appear to have been intended as parts a - e of 14.29. It should be possible to match answers with questions for your particular numbering system. I am giving all of the answers, because at the moment I can't check on exactly what the final printing will have.)

14.30 Intraclass correlation:

$$IC = \frac{MS_{subjects} - MS_{J \times S}}{MS_{subjects} + (j-1)MS_{J \times S} + j(MS_{Judge} - MS_{J \times S})/n}$$

$$= \frac{82.57 - 4.08}{82.57 + 2(4.08) + 3(70.12 - 4.08)/20}$$

$$= \frac{78.49}{82.57 + 8.16 + 6.30} = .85$$

The remainder of this exercise raises some questions that anyone interested in the reliability of their data (and we all *should* be) needs to be prepared to answer.

14.31 Differences due to Judges play an important role.

14.32 I would leave the variability due to Judge out of my calculations entirely.

14.33 If I was particularly interested in differences between subjects, and recognized that judges probably didn't have a good anchoring point, and if this lack was not meaningful, I would not be interested in considering it.

Chapter 15 - Multiple Regression

15.1 Predicting Quality of Life:

a. All other variables held constant, a difference of +1 degree in Temperature is associated with a difference of −.01 in perceived Quality of Life. A difference of $1000 in median Income, again all other variables held constant, is associated with a +.05 difference in perceived Quality of Life. A similar interpretation applies to b_3 and b_4. Since values of 0.00 cannot reasonably occur for all predictors, the intercept has no meaningful interpretation.

b. $\hat{Y} = 5.37 - .01(55) + .05(12) + .003(500) - .01(200) = 4.92$

c. $\hat{Y} = 5.37 - .01(55) + .05(12) + .003(100) - .01(200) = 3.72$

15.3 The F values for the four regression coefficients would be as follows:

$$F_1 = \left[\frac{\beta_1}{s_{\beta_1}}\right]^2 = \left[\frac{-0.438}{0.397}\right]^2 = 1.22 \qquad F_2 = \left[\frac{\beta_2}{s_{\beta_2}}\right]^2 = \left[\frac{0.762}{0.252}\right]^2 = 9.14$$

$$F_3 = \left[\frac{\beta_3}{s_{\beta_3}}\right]^2 = \left[\frac{0.081}{0.052}\right]^2 = 2.43 \qquad F_4 = \left[\frac{\beta_4}{s_{\beta_4}}\right]^2 = \left[\frac{-0.132}{0.025}\right]^2 = 27.88$$

I would thus delete Temperature, since it has the smallest F, and therefore the smallest semi-partial correlation with the dependent variable.

15.5 **a.** Envir has the largest semi-partial correlation with the criterion, because it has the largest value of t.

b. The gain in prediction (from $r = .58$ to $R = .697$) which we obtain by using all the predictors is more than offset by the loss of power we sustain as p became large relative to N.

15.7 As the correlation between two variables decreases, the amount of variance in a third variable that they share decreases. Thus the higher will be the possible squared semi-partial correlation of each variable with the criterion. They each can account for more previously unexplained variation.

15.9 The tolerance column shows us that NumSup and Respon are fairly well correlated with the other predictors, whereas Yrs is nearly independent of them.

15.11 Using Y and $\hat{Y}$ from Exercise 15.10:

$$MS_{residual} = \frac{\Sigma(Y-\hat{Y})^2}{(N-p-1)}$$

$$= \frac{42.322}{15-4-1} = 4.232 \quad \text{[as also calculated by BMDP in Exercise 15.4]}$$

15.13 Adjusted R^2 for 15 cases in Exercise 15.12:

$$R^2_{0.1234} = .173$$

$$\text{est } R^{*2} = 1 - \frac{(1-R^2)(N-1)}{(N-p-1)} = 1 - \frac{(1-.173)(14)}{(15-4-1)} = -.158$$

Since a squared value cannot be negative, we will declare it undefined. This is all the more reasonable in light of the fact that we cannot reject $H_0:R^* = 0$.

15.15 Using the first three variables from Exercise 15.4:

a. Figure comparable to Figure 15.1:

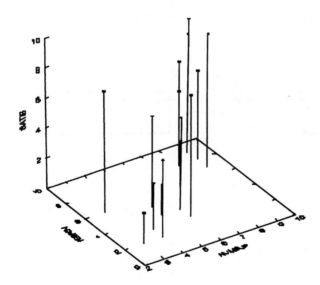

b. $\hat{Y} = 0.4067\text{Respon} + 0.1845\text{NumSup} + 2.3542$

The slope of the plane with respect to the Respon axis (X_1) = .4067
The slope of the plane with respect to the NumSup axis (X_2) = .1845
The plane intersects the Y axis at 2.3542

15.17 It has no meaning in that we have the data for the population of interest (the 10 districts).

15.19 It plays a major role through its correlation with the residual components of the other variables.

15.21 Within the context of a multiple-regression equation, we cannot look at one variable alone. The slope for one variable is only the slope for that variable when all other variables are held constant. The percentage of mothers not seeking care until the third trimester is correlated with a number of other variables.

15.23 Create set of data examining residuals.

15.25 Rerun of Exercise 15.24 adding PVTotal.

Adding PVTotal to the model does not improve the fit. R^2 increased by only .0001 and the standard error actually went up. The standard error for PVLoss jumped dramatically, from .1049 to .1777. This can be attributed to the fact that PVTotal was highly correlated with PVLoss.

15.27 Path diagram showing the relationships among the variables in the model.

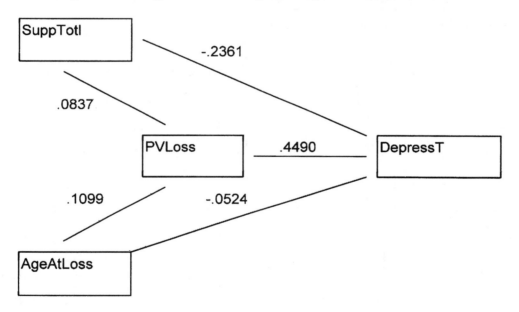

15.29 Regression diagnostics.

Case # 104 has the largest value of Cook's D (.137) but not a very large Studentized residual ($t = -1.88$). When we delete this case the squared multiple correlation is increased slightly. More importantly, the standard error of regression and the standard error of one of the predictors (PVLoss) also decrease slightly. This case is not sufficiently extreme to have a major impact on the data.

15.31 Logistic regression using Harass.dat:

The dependent variable (Reporting) is the last variable in the data set.

I cannot provide all possible models, so I am including just the most complete. This is a less than optimal model, but it provides a good starting point. This result was given by SPSS.

Block 1: Method = Enter

Omnibus Tests of Model Coefficients

		Chi-square	df	Sig.
Step 1	Step	35.442	5	.000
	Block	35.442	5	.000
	Model	35.442	5	.000

Model Summary

Step	-2 Log likelihood	Cox & Snell R Square	Nagelkerke R Square
1	439.984	.098	.131

Classification Table[a]

			Predicted		
			REPORT		Percentage
	Observed		No	Yes	Correct
Step 1	REPORT	No	111	63	63.8
		Yes	77	92	54.4
	Overall Percentage				59.2

a. The cut value is .500

Variables in the Equation

		B	S.E.	Wald	df	Sig.	Exp(B)
Step 1[a]	AGE	-.014	.013	1.126	1	.289	.986
	MARSTAT	-.072	.234	.095	1	.757	.930
	FEMIDEOL	.007	.015	.228	1	.633	1.007
	FREQBEH	-.046	.153	.093	1	.761	.955
	OFFENSIV	.488	.095	26.431	1	.000	1.629
	Constant	-1.732	1.430	1.467	1	.226	.177

a. Variable(s) entered on step 1: AGE, MARSTAT, FEMIDEOL, FREQBEH, OFFENSIV.

From this set of predictors we see that overall $\chi^2_{LR} = 35.44$, which is significant on 5 *df* with a *p* value of .0000 (to 4 decimal places). The only predictor that contributes significantly is the Offensiveness of the behavior, which has a Wald χ^2 of 26.43. The exponentiation of the regression coefficient yields 0.9547. This would suggest that as the offensiveness of the behavior increases, the likelihood of reporting *decreases*. That's an odd result. But remember that we have all variables in the model. If we simply predicting reporting by using Offensiveness, exp(B) = 1.65, which means that a 1 point increase in Offensiveness multiplies the odds of reporting by 1.65. Obviously we have some work to do to make sense of these data. I leave that to you.

15.33 It may well be that the frequency of the behavior is tied in with its offensiveness, which is related to the likelihood of reporting. In fact, the correlation between those two variables is .20, which is significant at $p < .000$. (I think my explanation would be more convincing if Frequency were a significant predictor when used on its own.)

15.35 I want students to think about what it means when we speak of "capitalizing on chance." You also should think about the fact that stepwise regression is a very atheoretical way of going about things, and perhaps theory should take more of a role.

15.37 You should see no change in the interaction term when you center the data, but you should see important differences in the "main effects" themselves. Look at the matrix of intercorrelations of the predictors.

Chapter 16 - Analyses of Variance and Covariance as General Linear Models

16.1   Eye fixations per line of text for poor, average, and good readers:

a. Design matrix, using only the first subject in each group:

$$X = \begin{bmatrix} 1 & 0 \\ 0 & 1 \\ -1 & -1 \end{bmatrix}$$

b. Computer exercise:

$R^2 = .608$ $SS_{reg} = 57.7333$ $SS_{residual} = 37.2000$

c. Analysis of variance:

$\bar{X}_1 = 8.2000$ $\bar{X}_2 = 5.6$ $\bar{X}_3 = 3.4$ $\bar{X}_. = 5.733$

$n_1 = 5$ $n_2 = 5$ $n_3 = 5$ $N = 15$ $\Sigma X = 86$ $\Sigma X^2 = 588$

$$SS_{total} = \Sigma X^2 - \frac{(\Sigma X)^2}{N} = 588 - \frac{86^2}{15} = 94.933$$

$$SS_{group} = n\Sigma\left(\bar{X}_j - \bar{X}_.\right)^2 = 5[(8.2000 - 5.733)^2 + (5.6 - 5.733)^2 + (3.4 - 5.733)^2]$$
$$= 57.733$$

$$SS_{error} = SS_{total} - SS_{group} = 94.933 - 57.733 = 37.200$$

Source	df	SS	MS	F
Group	2	57.733	28.867	9.312*
Error	12	37.200	3.100	
Total	14	94.933		

*$p < .05$ $[F_{.05(2,12)} = 3.89]$

16.3   Data from Exercise 16.1, modified to make unequal ns:

$R^2 = .624$ $SS_{reg} = 79.0095$ $SS_{residual} = 47.6571$

Analysis of variance:

$\bar{X}_1 = 8.2000$ $\bar{X}_2 = 5.8571$ $\bar{X}_3 = 3.3333$ $\bar{X}_. = 5.7968$

$$n_1 = 5 \quad n_2 = 7 \quad n_3 = 9 \quad N = 21 \quad \Sigma X = 112 \quad \Sigma X^2 = 724$$

$$SS_{total} = \Sigma X^2 - \frac{(\Sigma X)^2}{N} = 724 - \frac{112^2}{21} = 126.6666$$

$$SS_{group} = \Sigma n_j \left(\overline{X}_j - \overline{X}_. \right)^2 = 5[(8.2000 - 5.7968)^2 + 7(5.8571 - 5.7968)^2 + 9(3.3333 - 5.7968)^2]$$
$$= 79.0095$$

$$SS_{error} = SS_{total} - SS_{group} = 126.6666 - 79.0095 = 47.6571$$

Source	df	SS	MS	F
Group	2	79.0095	39.5048	14.92*
Error	18	47.6571	2.6476	
Total	20	126.6666		

$*p < .05 \quad [F_{.05(2,18)} = 3.55]$

16.5 Relationship between Gender, SES, and Locus of Control:

a. Analysis of Variance:

		SES			
		Low	Average	High	Mean
Gender	Male	12.25	14.25	17.25	14.583
	Female	8.25	12.25	16.25	12.250
	Mean	10.25	13.25	16.75	13.417

$$\Sigma X = 644 \qquad \Sigma X^2 = 9418 \quad n = 8 \quad N = 48$$

$$SS_{total} = \Sigma X^2 - \frac{(\Sigma X)^2}{N} = 9418 - \frac{644^2}{48} = 777.6667$$

$$SS_{gender} = sn\Sigma \left(\overline{X}_{i.} - \overline{X}_{..} \right)^2 = 3(8)[(14.583 - 13.417)^2 + (12.250 - 13.417)^2]$$
$$= 65.333$$

$$SS_{SES} = gn\Sigma \left(\overline{X}_{.j} - \overline{X}_{..} \right)^2 = 2(8)[(10.25 - 13.417)^2 + (13.25 - 13.417)^2 + (16.75 - 13.417)^2]$$
$$= 338.6667$$

$$SS_{cells} = n\Sigma \left(\overline{X}_{ij} - \overline{X}_{..} \right)^2 = 8[(12.25 - 13.417)^2 + ... + (16.25 - 13.417)^2] = 422.6667$$

$$SS_{GS} = SS_{cells} - SS_{gender} - SS_{SES} = 422.6667 - 65.3333 - 338.6667 = 18.6667$$

$$SS_{error} = SS_{total} - SS_{cells} = 777.6667 - 422.6667 = 355.0000$$

Source	df	SS	MS	F
Gender	1	65.333	65.333	7.730*
SES	2	338.667	169.333	20.034*
G x S	2	18.667	9.333	1.104
Error	42	355.000	8.452	
Total	47	777.667		

$*p < .05 \quad [F_{.05(1,42)} = 4.08; \; F_{.05(2,42)} = 3.23]$

b. ANOVA summary table constructed from sums of squares calculated from design matrix:

$$SS_G = SS_{reg(\alpha,\beta,\alpha\beta)} - SS_{reg(\beta,\alpha\beta)} = 422.6667 - 357.3333 = 65.333$$

$$SS_S = SS_{reg(\alpha,\beta,\alpha\beta)} - SS_{reg(\alpha,\alpha\beta)} = 422.6667 - 84.0000 = 338.667$$

$$SS_{GS} = SS_{reg(\alpha,\beta,\alpha\beta)} - SS_{reg(\alpha,\beta)} = 422.6667 - 404.000 = 18.667$$

$$SS_{total} = SS_Y = 777.667$$

The summary table is exactly the same as in part a (above).

16.7 The data from Exercise 16.5 modified to make unequal ns:

$$SS_{error} = SS_Y - SS_{reg(\alpha,\beta,\alpha\beta)} = 750.1951 - 458.7285 = 291.467$$

$$SS_G = SS_{reg(\alpha,\beta,\alpha\beta)} - SS_{reg(\beta,\alpha\beta)} = 458.7285 - 398.7135 = 60.015$$

$$SS_S = SS_{reg(\alpha,\beta,\alpha\beta)} - SS_{reg(\alpha,\alpha\beta)} = 458.7285 - 112.3392 = 346.389$$

$$SS_{GS} = SS_{reg(\alpha,\beta,\alpha\beta)} - SS_{reg(\alpha,\beta)} = 458.7285 - 437.6338 = 21.095$$

Source	df	SS	MS	F
Gender	1	60.015	60.015	7.21*
SES	2	346.389	173.195	20.80*
G x S	2	21.095	10.547	1.27
Error	35	291.467	8.328	
Total	40			

$*p < .05 \quad [F_{.05(1,35)} = 4.12; \; F_{.05(2,35)} = 3.27]$

16.9 Model from data in Exercise 16.5:

$$1.1667A_1 - 3.1667B_1 - 0.1667B_2 + 0.8333AB_{11} - 0.1667AB_{12} + 13.4167$$

Means:

		SES (B)				
		Low	Avg	High		
Gender (A)	Male	12.25	14.25	17.25	14.583	
	Female	8.25	12.25	16.25	12.250	
		10.25	13.25	16.75	13.417	

$$\hat{\mu} = \overline{X}.. = 13.4167 = b_0 = \text{intercept}$$

$$\hat{\alpha}_1 = \overline{A}_1 - \overline{X}.. = 14.583 - 13.4167 = 1.1667 = b_1$$

$$\hat{\beta}_1 = \overline{B}_1 - \overline{X}.. = 10.25 - 13.4167 = -3.1667 = b_2$$

$$\hat{\beta}_2 = \overline{B}_2 - \overline{X}.. = 13.25 - 13.4167 = -0.1667 = b_3$$

$$\hat{\alpha\beta}_{11} = \overline{AB}_{11} - \overline{A}_1 - \overline{B}_1 + \overline{X}.. = 12.25 - 14.583 - 10.25 + 13.4167 = 0.8337 = b_4$$

$$\hat{\alpha\beta}_{12} = \overline{AB}_{12} - \overline{A}_1 - \overline{B}_2 + \overline{X}.. = 14.25 - 14.583 - 13.250 + 13.4167 = -0.1667 = b_5$$

16.11 Does Method I really deal with unweighted means?

Means:

	B_1	B_2	weighted	unweighted
A_1	4	10	8.5	7.0
A_2	10	4	8.0	7.0
weighted	8.0	8.5	8.29	
unweighted	7.0	7.0		7.0

The full model produced by Method 1: $\hat{Y} = 0.0A_1 + 0.0B_1 - 3.0AB_{11} + 7.0$

Effects calculated on weighted means:

$$\hat{\mu} = \overline{X}. = 8.29 \neq b_0 = \text{intercept}$$

$$\hat{\alpha}_1 = \overline{A}_1 - \overline{X}. = 8.5 - 8.29 = .21 \neq b_1$$

$$\hat{\beta}_1 = \overline{B}_1 - \overline{X}. = 8.0 - 8.29 = -.29 \neq b_2$$

$$\hat{\alpha\beta}_{11} = \overline{AB}_{11} - \overline{A}_1 - \overline{B}_1 + \overline{X}. = 4.00 - 8.5 - 8.0 + 8.29 = -4.21 \neq b_3$$

Effects calculated on unweighted means:

$$\hat{\mu} = \overline{X}_{..} = 7.00 = b_0 = \text{intercept}$$

$$\hat{\alpha}_1 = \overline{A}_1 - \overline{X}_{..} = 7.0 - 7.0 = 0.0 = b_1$$

$$\hat{\beta}_1 = \overline{B}_1 - \overline{X}_{..} = 7.0 - 7.0 = 0.0 = b_2$$

$$\hat{\alpha\beta}_{11} = \overline{AB}_{11} - \overline{A}_1 - \overline{B}_1 + \overline{X}_{..} = 4.00 - 7.0 - 7.0 + 7.0 = -3.0 = b_3$$

These coefficients found by the model clearly reflect the effects computed on unweighted means. Alternately, carrying out the complete analysis leads to $SS_A = SS_B = 0.00$, again reflecting equality of unweighted means.

16.13 Venn diagram representing the sums of squares in Exercise 16.7:

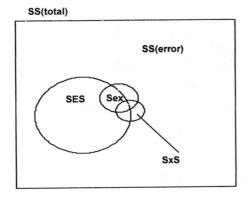

16.15 Energy consumption of families:

a. Design matrix, using only the first entry in each group for illustration purposes:

$$X = \begin{bmatrix} 1 & 0 & 58 & 75 \\ \dots & \dots & \dots & \dots \\ 0 & 1 & 60 & 70 \\ \dots & \dots & \dots & \dots \\ -1 & -1 & 75 & 80 \end{bmatrix}$$

b. Analysis of covariance:

$$SS_{reg(\alpha,cov,\alpha c)} = 2424.6202$$

$$SS_{reg(\alpha,cov)} = 2369.2112$$

$$SS_{residual} = 246.5221 = SS_{error}$$

There is not a significant decrement in SS_{reg} and thus we can continue to assume homogeneity of regression.

$$SS_{reg(\alpha)} = 1118.5333$$

$$SS_{cov} = SS_{reg(\alpha,cov)} - SS_{reg(\alpha)} = 2369.2112 - 1118.5333 = 1250.6779$$

$$SS_{reg(cov)} = 1716.2884$$

$$SS_A = SS_{reg(\alpha,cov)} - SS_{reg(cov)} = 2369.2112 - 1716.2884 = 652.9228$$

Source	df	SS	MS	F
Covariate	1	1250.6779	1250.6779	55.81*
A (Group)	2	652.9228	326.4614	14.57*
Error	11	246.5221	22.4111	
Total	14	2615.7333		

$*p < .05$ $[F_{.05(1,11)} = 4.84; F_{.05(2,11)} = 3.98]$

16.17 Adjusted means for the data in Exercise 16.16:

(The order of the means may differ depending on how you code the group membership and how the software sets up its design matrix. But the numerical values should agree.)

$$\hat{Y} = -7.9099A_1 + 0.8786A_2 - 2.4022B + 0.5667AB_{11} + 0.1311AB_{21} + 0.7260C + 6.3740$$

$$\hat{Y}_{11} = -7.9099(1) + 0.8786(0) - 2.4022(1) + 0.5667(1) + 0.1311(0)$$
$$+ 0.7260(61.3333) + 6.3740 = 41.1566$$

$$\hat{Y}_{12} = -7.9099(1) + 0.8786(0) - 2.4022(-1) + 0.5667(-1) + 0.1311(0)$$
$$+ 0.7260(61.3333) + 6.3740 = 44.8276$$

$$\hat{Y}_{21} = -7.9099(0) + 0.8786(1) - 2.4022(1) + 0.5667(0) + 0.1311(1)$$
$$+ 0.7260(61.3333) + 6.3740 = 49.5095$$

$$\hat{Y}_{22} = -7.9099(0) + 0.8786(1) - 2.4022(-1) + 0.5667(0) + 0.1311(-1)$$
$$+ 0.7260(61.3333) + 6.3740 = 54.0517$$

$$\hat{Y}_{31} = -7.9099(-1) + 0.8786(-1) - 2.4022(1) + 0.5667(-1) + 0.1311(-1)$$
$$+ 0.7260(61.3333) + 6.3740 = 54.8333$$

$$\hat{Y}_{32} = -7.9099(-1) + 0.8786(-1) - 2.4022(-1) + 0.5667(1) + 0.1311(1)$$
$$+ 0.7260(61.3333) + 6.3740 = 61.0333$$

(We enter 61.3333 for the covariate in each case, because we want to estimate what the cell means would be if the observations in those cells were always at the mean of the covariate.)

16.19 Computer exercise.

16.21 Analysis of GSIT in Mireault.dat:

Tests of Between-Subjects Effects

Dependent Variable: GSIT

Source	Type III Sum of Squares	df	Mean Square	F	Sig.
Corrected Model	1216.924[a]	5	243.385	2.923	.013
Intercept	1094707.516	1	1094707.516	13146.193	.000
GENDER	652.727	1	652.727	7.839	.005
GROUP	98.343	2	49.172	.590	.555
GENDER * GROUP	419.722	2	209.861	2.520	.082
Error	30727.305	369	83.272		
Total	1475553.000	375			
Corrected Total	31944.229	374			

a. R Squared = .038 (Adjusted R Squared = .025)

Estimated Marginal Means

GENDER * GROUP

Dependent Variable: GSIT

GENDER	GROUP	Mean	Std. Error	95% Confidence Interval Lower Bound	Upper Bound
Male	1	62.367	1.304	59.804	64.931
	2	64.676	1.107	62.500	66.853
	3	63.826	1.903	60.084	67.568
Female	1	62.535	.984	60.600	64.470
	2	60.708	.858	59.020	62.396
	3	58.528	1.521	55.537	61.518

16.23 Analysis of variance on the covariate from Exercise 16.22.

The following is abbreviated SAS output.

General Linear Models Procedure

Dependent Variable: YEARCOLL

Source	DF	Sum of Squares	Mean Square	F Value	Pr > F
Model	5	13.3477645	2.6695529	2.15	0.0600
Error	292	363.0012288	1.2431549		
Corrected Total	297	376.3489933			

R-Square	C.V.	Root MSE	YEARCOLL Mean
0.035466	41.53258	1.11497	2.6845638

Source	DF	Type III SS	Mean Square	F Value	Pr > F
GENDER	1	5.95006299	5.95006299	4.79	0.0295
GROUP	2	0.78070431	0.39035216	0.31	0.7308
GENDER*GROUP	2	2.96272310	1.48136155	1.19	0.3052

GENDER	GROUP	YEARCOLL LSMEAN
1	1	2.27906977
1	2	2.53225806
1	3	2.68421053
2	1	2.88888889
2	2	2.85000000
2	3	2.70967742

These data reveal a significant difference between males and females in terms of YearColl. Females are slightly ahead of males. If the first year of college is in fact more stressful than later years, this could account for some of the difference we found in Exercise 16.21.

16.25 One of the most obvious problems is that males and females differed substantially on condom use at pretest. Adjusting for pretest differences would indirectly control for Gender, which is not something we are likely to want to do.

Chapter 17 - Log-Linear Analysis

17.1 Possible models for data on idiomatic communication.

$\ln(F_{ij}) = \lambda$ *Equiprobability*

$\ln(F_{ij}) = \lambda + \lambda^F$ *Conditional equiprobability on Function*

$\ln(F_{ij}) = \lambda + \lambda^I$ *Conditional equiprobability on Inventor*

$\ln(F_{ij}) = \lambda + \lambda^F + \lambda^I$ *Independence*

$\ln(F_{ij}) = \lambda + \lambda^F + \lambda^I + \lambda^{FI}$ *Saturated model*

17.3 Lambda values for the complete (saturated) model.

a. $\lambda = 2.8761 = $ mean of $\ln\left(\text{cell}_{ij}\right)$

b. $\lambda^{\text{Inventor}} = .199 \quad .540 \quad -.739$

The effect for "female partner" is .199, indicating that the ln(frequencies in row 1) are slightly above average.

c. $\lambda^{\text{Function}} = -.632 \quad .260 \quad .222 \quad -.007 \quad .097 \quad -.667 \quad .303 \quad -.029 \quad .452$

The effect of Confrontation is -.632. Confrontation contributes somewhat less than its share of idiosyncratic expressions.

d. $\lambda^{\text{Inventor + Function}} = $

.196	−.039	...	.249	.028
−.481	.038	...	.250	.259
.286	.001	...	−.500	−.287

The unique effect of cell_{11} is .196. It contributes slightly more than would be predicted from the row and column totals above.

17.5 For females the odds in favor of a direct hit are 6.00, whereas for males they are only 2.8125. This leaves an odds ratio of 6.00/2.8125 = 2.1333. A female is 2.1333 times more likely to have a direct hit than a male.

17.7 Letting S represent Satisfaction, G represent Gender, and V represent Validity, and with 0.50 added to all cells because of small frequencies, the optimal model is

$$\ln(Fij) = \lambda + \lambda^G + \lambda^S + \lambda^V + \lambda^{SV}$$

For this model $\chi^2 = 4.53$ on 5 *df*; *p* = .4763

An appropriate model for these data must take into account differences due to Satisfaction, Gender, and Validity. It must also take into account differences associated with a Satisfaction × Validity interaction. However, there are not relationships involving any of the other interactions.

17.9 Compare statistics from alternative designs:

The student should examine the pattern of changes in the alternative designs. Although the marginal frequencies stay constant from design to design, the chi-square tests on those effects, the values of λ, and the tests on λ change as variables are added. This differs from what we see in the analysis of variance, where sums of squares remain unchanged as we look at additional independent variables (all other things equal).

17.11 Odds of being classed as adult delinquent.

Odds delinquent:
Normal Testosterone, Low SES   =   190/1104 = .1721
High Testosterone, Low SES   =   62/140 = .4429
Normal Testosterone, High SES =   53/1114 = .0476
High Testosterone, High SES   =   3/70 = .0429

17.13 Optimal model for Dabbs and Morris (1990) Testosterone data.

The following is an SPSS program and the resulting output. The optimal model that results is one including all main effects and first order interactions, but not the three-way interactions. The value of χ^2 for this model is 3.52 on 1 df, for p = .0607. If any main effect or interaction were dropped from the model, the χ^2 would be significant. The parameter estimates are based on the saturated model—the standard SPSS approach.

(*Note:* To reproduce the following results using SPSS 10.0, chose **Loglinear/Model Selection**, and select Display Parameter Estimates from the Options dialog box.)

```
TITLE  'SPSS loglinear analysis on Testosterone Data'
FILE HANDLE DATA /NAME = '[d_howell.book]Testost.dat'
DATA LIST FILE = DATA  Free
                       / SES Delinq Testost Freq
Weight by Freq
Value labels   SES 1 'Low' 2 'High'/
               Delinq 1 'Yes' 2 'No'/
               Testost 1 'Normal' 2 'High'/
Hiloglinear    SES (1,2)Delinq (1,2) Testost (1,2)/
               Print Estim, Association/
               Design=SES*Delinq*Testost/
               Design=SES*Delinq SES*Testost Delinq*Testost/
```

Note: For saturated models   0.500 has been added to all observed cells.
      Goodness-of-fit test statistics

                Likelihood ratio chi square =   .00000 DF = 0 P = 1.000
                        Pearson chi square =   .00000 DF = 0 P = 1.000

- -
      Tests that K-way and higher order effects are zero.

K	DF	L.R. Chisq	Prob	Pearson Chisq	Prob	Iteration
3	1	3.518	.0607	2.988	.0839	3
2	4	185.825	.0000	218.034	.0000	2
1	7	4085.232	.0000	4653.105	.0000	0

- -
Tests that K-way effects are zero.

K	DF	L.R. Chisq	Prob	Pearson Chisq	Prob	Iteration
1	3	3899.407	.0000	4435.071	.0000	0
2	3	182.307	.0000	215.046	.0000	0
3	1	3.518	.0607	2.988	.0839	0

Effect Name	DF	Partial Chisq	Prob	Iter
SES*DELINQ	1	98.559	.0000	2
SES*TESTOST	1	31.678	.0000	2
DELINQ*TESTOST	1	24.380	.0000	2
SES	1	23.988	.0000	2
DELINQ	1	1867.516	.0000	2
TESTOST	1	2007.903	.0000	2

- -

Estimates for Parameters.

SES*DELINQ*TESTOST

Parameter	Coeff.	Std. Err.	Z-Value	Lower 95 CI	Upper 95 CI
1	-.1142281423	.07382	-1.54739	-.25892	.03046

SES*DELINQ

Parameter	Coeff.	Std. Err.	Z-Value	Lower 95 CI	Upper 95 CI
1	.4339740600	.07382	5.87883	.28929	.57866

SES*TESTOST

Parameter	Coeff.	Std. Err.	Z-Value	Lower 95 CI	Upper 95 CI
1	-.2888801196	.07382	-3.91331	-.43357	-.14419

DELINQ*TESTOST

Parameter	Coeff.	Std. Err.	Z-Value	Lower 95 CI	Upper 95 CI
1	-.1226355817	.07382	-1.66128	-.26732	.02205

SES

Parameter	Coeff.	Std. Err.	Z-Value	Lower 95 CI	Upper 95 CI
1	.6041194722	.07382	8.18370	.45943	.74881

DELINQ

Parameter	Coeff.	Std. Err.	Z-Value	Lower 95 CI	Upper 95 CI
1	-1.075858250	.07382	-14.57410	-1.22055	-.93117

TESTOST

Parameter	Coeff.	Std. Err.	Z-Value	Lower 95 CI	Upper 95 CI
1	1.0829866625	.0738	14.67067	.93830	1.22767

```
* * * * *  H I E R A R C H I C A L   L O G   L I N E A R  * * * *
DESIGN 2 has generating class
    SES*DELINQ
    SES*TESTOST
    DELINQ*TESTOST
- - - - - - - - - - - - - - - - - - - - - - - - - - - - - - - -
Goodness-of-fit test statistics
            Likelihood ratio chi square =    3.51824 DF = 1  P =    .061
                    Pearson chi square =    2.98809 DF = 1  P =    .084
- - - - - - - - - - - - - - - - - - - - - - - - - - - - - - - -
```

17.15 The complete solution for Pugh's (1984) data would take pages to present. Pugh selected the model that includes Fault*Verdict and Gender*Moral*verdict. This model has a $\chi^2 = 6.71$ on 10 df, with an associated probability of .7529. This is the model that BMDP4F would select if you chose a significance level of .15 for your cutoff.

Pugh (1984) derived his potential solutions from a theoretical analysis of the hypotheses. He tested the following models and obtained the accompanying χ^2 statistics. It would be instructive for students to compare these theoretically tested models against standard approaches to model building.

Model	Test of Fit			Added Effect Difference		
	df	χ^2	p	df	χ^2	p
GM,F,V	16	70.98	<.001			
GM,GF,V	15	70.93	<.001	1	.05	>.05
GM,GF,MF,V	13	68.06	<.001	2	2.87	>.05
GM,GF,MF,FV	12	32.68	<.01	1	35.38	<.001
GM,GF,MF,FV,GV	11	23.16	<.02	1	9.52	<.01
GM,GF,MF,FV,GV,MV	9	15.07	>.05	2	8.09	<.02
GM,MF,FV,GMV	7	3.71	>.05	2	11.36	<.01
GMV,GMF,GFV,MFV	2	2.94	>.05	5	0.77	>.05
FV,GMV	10	6.71	>.05	3	3.00	>.05

Chapter 18 – Resampling and Nonparametric Approaches to Data

18.1 Inferences in children's story summaries (McConaughy, 1980):

a. Analysis using Wilcoxon's rank-sum test:

	Younger Children							Older Children					
Raw Data:	0	1	0	3	2	5	2		4	7	6	4	8	7
Ranks:	1.5	3	1.5	6	4.5	9	4.5		7.5	11.5	10	7.5	13	11.5

$$\sum R = 30 \qquad N = 7 \qquad\qquad \sum R = 61 \qquad N = 6$$

$$W_S = \Sigma R \text{ for group with smaller } N = 61$$
$$W_S' = 2\,\overline{W} - W_S = 84 - 61 = 23$$

$W'_S < W_S$, therefore use W'_S in Appendix W_S. Double the probability level for a 2-tailed test.

$$W_{.025\,(6,7)} = 27 > 23$$

b. Reject H_0 and conclude that older children include more inferences in their summaries.

18.3 The analysis in Exercise 18.2 using the normal approximation:

$$z = \frac{W_S - \dfrac{n_1(n_1 + n_2 + 1)}{2}}{\sqrt{\dfrac{n_1 n_2 (n_1 + n_2 + 1)}{12}}} = \frac{53 - \dfrac{9(9 + 11 + 1)}{2}}{\sqrt{\dfrac{9(11)(9 + 11 + 1)}{12}}} = -3.15$$

z	p
3.00	.0013
3.15	.0009
3.25	.0006

$$p(z \geq \pm 3.15) = 2(.0009) = .0018 < .05$$

Reject H_0, which was the same conclusion as we came to in Exercise 18.2.

18.5 Hypothesis formation in psychiatric residents (Nurcombe & Fitzhenry-Coor, 1979):

a. Analysis using Wilcoxon's matched-pairs signed-ranks test:

Before:	8	4	2	2	4	8	3	1	3	9
After:	7	9	3	6	3	10	6	7	8	7
Difference:	-1	+5	+1	+4	-1	+2	+3	+6	+5	-2
Rank:	2	8.5	2	7	2	4.5	6	10	8.5	4.5

| Signed | | 8.5 | 2 | 7 | | 4.5 | 6 | 10 | 8.5 |
| Rank: | -2 | | | | -2 | | | | -4.5 |

$$T_+ = \Sigma(\text{positive ranks}) = 46.5$$

$$T_- = \Sigma(\text{negative ranks}) = 8.5$$

$T = \text{smaller of } |T_+| \text{ or } |T_-| = 8.5$

$T_{.025\,(10)} = 8 < 8.5$ Do not reject H_0.

b. We cannot conclude that we have evidence supporting the hypothesis that there is a reliable increase in hypothesis generation and testing over time. (Here is a case in which alternative methods of breaking ties could lead to different conclusions.)

18.7 I would randomly assign the two scores for each subject to the Before and After location, and calculate my test statistic (the sum of the negative differences) for each randomization. Having done that a large number of times, the distribution of the sum of negative differences would be the sampling distribution against which to compare my obtained result.

18.9 The analysis in Exercise 18.8 using the normal approximation:

$$z = \frac{T - \dfrac{n(n+1)}{4}}{\sqrt{\dfrac{n(n+1)(2n+1)}{24}}} = \frac{46 - \dfrac{20(20+1)}{4}}{\sqrt{\dfrac{20(20+1)(40+1)}{24}}} = -2.20$$

$$p(z \geq \pm 2.20) = 2(.0139) = .0278 < .05$$

Again reject H_0, which agrees with our earlier conclusion.

18.11   Data in Exercise 18.8 plotted as a function of first-born's score:

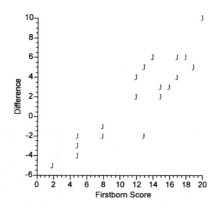

The scatter plot shows that the difference between the pairs is heavily dependent upon the score for the first born.

112

18.13 The Wilcoxon matched-pairs signed-ranks test tests the null hypothesis that paired scores were drawn from identical populations or from symmetric populations with the same mean (and median). The corresponding t test tests the null hypothesis that the paired scores were drawn from populations with the same mean and assumes normality.

18.15 Rejection of H_0 by a t test is a more specific statement than rejection using the appropriate distribution-free test because, by making assumptions about normality and homogeneity of variance, the t test refers specifically to population means.

18.17 Truancy and home situation of delinquent adolescents:

Analysis using Kruskal-Wallis one-way analysis of variance:

Natural Home		Foster Home		Group Home	
Score	Rank	Score	Rank	Score	Rank
15	18	16	19	10	9
18	22	14	16	13	13.5
19	24.5	20	26	14	16
14	16	22	27	11	10
5	4.5	19	24.5	7	6.5
8	8	5	4.5	3	2
12	11.5	17	20	4	3
13	13.5	18	22	18	22
7	6.5	12	11.5	2	1
$R_i =$	124.5		170.5		83

$N = 27 \qquad n = 9$

$$H = \frac{12}{N(N+1)} \Sigma \frac{R_i^2}{n_i} - 3(N+1)$$

$$= \frac{12}{27(27+1)} \left[\frac{124.5^2}{9} + \frac{170.5^2}{9} + \frac{83^2}{9} \right] - 3(27+1)$$

$$= 6.757$$

$$\chi_{.05}^2(2) = 5.99 \quad \text{Do not reject } H_0$$

18.19 I would take the data from all of the groups and assign them at random to the groups. For each random assignment I would calculate a statistic that reflected the differences (or lack thereof) among the groups. The standard F statistic would be a good one to use. This randomization, repeated many times, will give me the sampling distribution of F, and that distribution does not depend on an assumption of normality. I could then compare the F that I obtained for my data against that sampling distribution.

18.21 The study in Exercise 18.18 has the advantage over the one in Exercise 18.17 in that it eliminates the influence of individual differences (differences in overall level of truancy from one person to another).

18.23 For the data in Exercise 18.5:

a. Analyzed by chi-square:

	More	Fewer	Total
Observed	7	3	10
Expected	5	5	10

$$\chi^2 = \Sigma \frac{(O-E)^2}{E}$$

$$= \frac{(7-5)^2}{5} + \frac{(3-5)^2}{5}$$

$$= 1.6 \qquad \left[\chi^2_{.05(1)} = 3.84\right] \qquad \text{Do not reject } H_0.$$

b. Analyzed by Friedman's test:

Before		After	
8	(2)	7	(1)
4	(1)	9	(2)
2	(1)	3	(2)
2	(1)	6	(2)
4	(2)	3	(1)
8	(1)	10	(2)
3	(1)	6	(2)
1	(1)	7	(2)
3	(1)	8	(2)
9	(2)	7	(1)
	(13)		(17)

$N = 10 \qquad k = 2$

$$\chi^2_F = \frac{12}{Nk(k+1)} \Sigma R_i^2 - 3N(k+1)$$

$$= \frac{12}{12(2)(2+1)}\left[13^2 + 17^2\right] - 3(10)(2+1)$$

$$= 1.6 \qquad \left[\chi^2_{.05}(2) = 5.99\right] \text{ Do not reject } H_0$$

These are exactly equivalent tests in this case.